Managing Successful
Programmes

Office of Government Commerce

LONDON: The Stationery Office

Edited, designed and typeset by Format Information Design.

British Library Cataloguing in Publication Data

First published 1999
Second impression 2001

ISBN 0 11 330016 6

For further information regarding this and other OGC products please contact:
OGC Service Desk
Rosebery Court
St Andrews Business Park
Norwich
NR7 0HS
Telephone: 0845 000 4999

Published by The Stationery Office and available from:

The Stationery Office
(mail, telephone and fax orders only)
PO Box 29, Norwich NR3 1GN
General enquiries/Telephone orders 0870 600 5522
Fax orders 0870 600 5533

www.thestationeryoffice.com

The Stationery Office Bookshops
123 Kingsway, London WC2B 6PQ
020 7242 6393 Fax 020 7242 6394
68-69 Bull Street, Birmingham B4 6AD
0121 236 9696 Fax 0121 236 9699
33 Wine Street, Bristol BS1 2BQ
0117 9264306 Fax 0117 929 4515
9-21 Princess Street, Manchester M60 8AS
0161 834 7201 Fax 0161 833 0634
16 Arthur Street, Belfast BT1 4GD
028 9023 8451 Fax 028 9023 5401
The Stationery Office Oriel Bookshop
18 19 High Street, Cardiff CF1 2BZ
029 2039 5548 Fax 029 2038 4347
71 Lothian Road, Edinburgh EH3 9AZ
0870 606 5566 Fax 0870 606 5588

The Stationery Office's Accredited Agents
(see Yellow Pages)

and through good booksellers

Printed in the United Kingdom for The Stationery Office
TJ4059 C25 4/01 10170

CONTENTS

Contents

Contents

LIST OF FIGURES

LIST OF TABLES

ACKNOWLEDGEMENTS

Calyx Consulting Ltd, under contract to the former CCTA (now OGC), is acknowledged for contributing the development material used within this guide. OGC would like to thank Tom Saunders of Calyx Consulting Ltd and Andrew Richards of Programme Consulting Ltd for their considerable help and input during the development of this guide.

OGC would also like to thank the members of the Programme Management Review Panel who kindly provided their expert views and comments throughout the development process. The Review Panel members are:

Organisation	Review Panel member
Andersen Consulting	Mitchell Leimon
Automobile Association	Sue Vowler
The BCS/APM Programme	
Management SIG	Geoff Reiss
Benefits Agency	Helen Howarth
Civil Service College	Peter Court
Customer Projects Limited	Eddie Borup
DMR Consulting Group	John Bartlett
DSS	Directorate for Project Management
Ernst & Young	John Cook
French Thornton	Tim O'Leary
GCHQ	John Wright
Home Office	Liz Sparrow
Human Systems Limited	Terry Cooke Davies
Inland Revenue	Roger Cully
MOD - DGICS	Kevin Gollogly
MOD (RN) - NSC	Pam Watson
MOD –RAF - LITS	Grp Capt Nick Morris
NAO	Nigel Salt
NatWest Bank	Jeff Matraves
NatWest Bank	Lloyd Richards
PA Consulting Group	Graeme Pateman
Parity	Derek Green
PriceWaterhouseCoopers	Richard Archer
Prison Service	Ingrid Posen
Prudential	The Projects Office
Touchstone Computers	John Chapman
Warburg Dillon Read	David Bowen

FOREWORD

How can we ensure success with major projects and programmes of business change? The combination of complexity, high risk and multiple projects can result in high profile failure without robust management.

Programme Management is a pragmatic approach that will help organisations deliver and realise the required benefits, innovation, and new ways of working that will take them through the next decade.

The general principles of Programme Management have been developed and applied in many different areas and for many years. They are equally applicable to complex projects such as the construction of major buildings and to business change programmes such as the exploitation of e-commerce and electronic service delivery.

This guide sets out OGC's approach to Programme Management, developed in coordination with public and private sector organisations. It addresses today's business environment and takes into account factors such as rapid change and the requirement for a number of organisations to work together.

I hope that the guidance will help you and your organisation in delivering successful programmes.

Bob Assirati
Executive Director, IT Directorate, Office of Government Commerce

one

INTRODUCTION

1.1 Background

Change is a way of life for all organisations. New types of business processes are being introduced, supplier relationships are changing, organisations merge and divide in response to political or market forces. Organisations are also striving to achieve benefits from improving existing practices, to achieve business excellence, to be better prepared for the future, to enable innovation and to encourage new ways of thinking about doing business. Where there is major change there will be complexity and risk. There could be many inter-dependencies and conflicting priorities to resolve. Programme Management provides a framework for the management of complexity and risk.

There may be a number of reasons for creating a programme. Some of the drivers for change are shown in Figure 1 together with the areas within organisations that may be affected as a result of the change. In order to achieve change, organisations must be

Figure 1:
The drivers for change

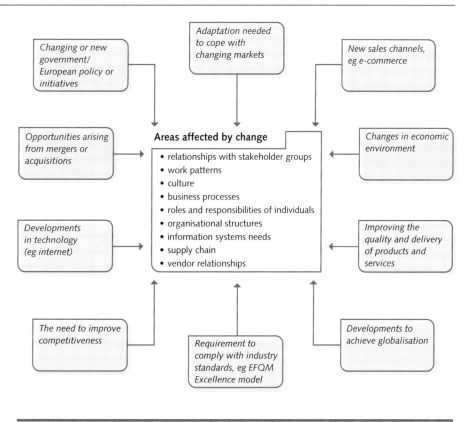

able to manage the path through the change process. However, the variety and pace of change in today's business environment can cause an overload of changes for those in the business environment, whose first priority is to keep the ongoing business operations running efficiently, economically and effectively, irrespective of change. Programme Management provides an organisation, a set of processes and outputs, and ways of thinking that together enable organisations to implement change and cope with the inherent problems and challenges.

1.2 Purpose of this guide

This guide describes OGC's recommended approach for managing programmes. Its purpose is to explain:

- the characteristics of programmes
- the concepts of Programme Management
- the main roles, activities, processes and products of the approach.

The approach described in this guide is not intended to be prescriptive. Circumstances will vary from organisation to organisation and from programme to programme. The best practice set out in this guide will need adaptation to suit the requirements of individual situations. However, certain principles are key to the successful management of all programmes and these are identified and discussed in this guide. Programme Management interfaces with Project Management. In this guide, references are made to PRINCE2, the structured method for managing projects developed by OGC. PRINCE2 covers the project lifecycle from start-up to closure covering Project Management process descriptions and techniques.

1.3 What is Programme Management?

> **Definition of Programme Management**
>
> Programme Management is the co-ordinated management of a portfolio of projects that change organisations to achieve benefits that are of strategic importance.

Programme Management brings related projects together to manage their inter-dependencies. It maintains a strategic view over the set of projects, aligning and co-ordinating them within a programme of business change in support of specific business strategies. It provides the linkage that connects individual projects to a rapidly changing business environment and constantly evolving strategy.

Programme Management provides the framework for implementing business strategies and initiatives, or large scale change, where there is a 'vision' of the programme's outcome – a transformed organisation, for example. The path to achieving this vision may deviate and change direction. The vision itself may require adapting as work progresses along the way. Programme Management helps to organise, manage, accommodate and control these changes such that the eventual outcome meets the objectives set by the business strategy.

Programme Management provides an organisation structure and process definitions that:

- enable linkage between the top level strategic direction of organisations and the management activities required to achieve strategic objectives
- ensures the goals of a programme remain valid in response to changes outside the programme
- supports senior managers who have to plan and control activities, set priorities and allocate resources for implementation of groups of related projects
- ensures the impact of changes on the organisations and stakeholders involved is managed and that the intended change is achieved in the optimum way
- enables the effective delegation and management of work through the execution of discrete projects
- ensures all issues are recognised and managed to maximise success
- ensures risks to the programme's successful completion are identified, monitored, managed and controlled in a way acceptable to management
- ensures all stakeholders are informed and involved and that their interests are appropriately considered
- helps to focus management attention clearly on the realisation of benefits that are defined and understood at the outset and achieved throughout the lifetime of the programme and beyond.

1.4 The benefits of Programme Management

Table 1 summaries the main benefits of Programme Management and identifies where they will take effect.

Table 1: *The benefits of Programme Management*	Area of impact	Benefit
	Delivery of change	More effective delivery of changes because the changes can be planned and implemented in an integrated way ensuring that current business operations are not adversely affected
	Alignment between strategy and project levels	Effective response to strategic initiatives by filling the gap between strategies and projects
	Management support	Keeping activities focused on the business change objectives by providing a framework for senior management to direct and manage the change process
	Resource management	More efficient management of resources by providing a mechanism for project prioritisation and project integration

Risk management	Better management of risk because the wider context is understood and explicitly acknowledged
Benefit realisation	Help to achieve real business benefits through a formal process of benefit identification, management, realisation and measurement
Management control	Improved control through a framework within which the costs of introducing new infrastructure, standards and quality regimes can be justified, measured and assessed
Business operations	Clarification of how new business operations will deliver improved performance by defining the desired benefits and linking these to the achievement of new working practices
Management of Business Case	More effective management of the Business Case by building and maintaining a Business Case that clearly compares current business operations with the more beneficial future business operations
Co-ordination and control	More efficient co-ordination and control of the often complex range of activities by clearly defining roles and responsibilities for managing the Project Portfolio and realising the benefits delivered by the programme
Transition management	Smooth transition from current to future business operations through the clear recognition and responsibility for preparing the organisation for migration to new ways of working
Consistency	Achieving a consistent system of new or amended policies, standards, and work practices through the integrated definition, planning, delivery and assurance of the required changes

1.5 When to use Programme Management

A Programme Management approach may be applied in different ways and with different emphasis. Programmes may be set up to implement change in parts of an organisation, in the whole organisation, or across a group of organisations.

Programme Management can be applied to all these situations to focus and direct the activities in order to achieve the maximum benefits. Table 2 shows some situations that are likely to benefit from a Programme Management approach.

Table 2: *When to use Programme Management*	Situation	How Programme Management helps
	Where there is complexity	to co-ordinate activities across many specialisms or business units
	Where there are design interfaces between projects	to harmonise design and preserve integrity
	Where resources are scarce	to set priorities and adjudicate between project conflicts
	Where there is potential for activities or products common to more than one project	to identify and exploit the opportunities for economies from sharing
	Where there is the probability of change during the running of the programme	to provide flexible information flows and facilitate top-down, well informed decision-making so that appropriate adjustments can be made
	Where there is uncertainty	to provide a framework for communication and to promote common values and shared responsibilities so as to foster collaboration from all the parties involved
	Where there is potential to develop a series of outcomes	to reap benefits early
	Where there is a requirement for improvement	to align and co-ordinate a range of continuous improvements to business operations and services
	Where there is high risk	to manage, monitor and reduce the risk to acceptable levels without impeding the successful outcome of the programme

1.6 Programme Management examples

Programme Management can be used where there are shared objectives across a number of projects or initiatives, for example, where:

- there is a need to co-ordinate several initiatives affecting one or more business areas

- a set of proposed projects supports a strategy, a strategic change or a similar type of initiative with significant impact on the organisation
- a set of proposed projects and activities addresses different parts of a common problem or is needed to deliver an overall business benefit
- more than one organisation enters into a joint collaboration or partnership arrangement to achieve major change affecting all participating organisations
- two or more organisations need to collaborate to achieve a required outcome.

Programme Management can be applied where there is *complexity* (and hence increased risk) of inter-relations between specialisms or groups of projects, such as where:
- the set of changes affects too wide a range of business areas or requires too many specialist development skills for a conventional Project Management organisation
- there are strong inter-dependencies between projects that require co-ordinated management.

Programme Management can enable more efficient utilisation of *shared resources*, such as where:
- the use of resources from a common pool can be optimised by co-ordination across projects
- resources are owned by different organisations and shared across the set of projects.

Programme Management can help *reduce costs* overall, for example, where:
- the grouping of projects gives cost savings by avoiding duplication of effort
- the grouping of projects provides the increase in scale to justify necessary infra-structure
- the grouping of projects justifies the employment, recruitment or training of specialist skills, which will be more than repaid through improved business operations
- the implementation activities stemming from two or more projects can be merged together.

1.7 Different types of programme

Programme Management concepts, techniques and processes bring benefits to the increasingly varied types of programme that need to be managed. However, as every project is unique so is every programme. There are many different types of programme that organisations may wish to manage and control using a Programme Management approach, each with its own particular set of objectives and desired benefits. Examples include:
- a *strategic programme* where multiple activities and projects are intended to move the organisation towards achieving a set of pre-defined objectives within an overall 'business drive'. Objectives may not always be totally compatible with each other and a continuing challenge may be how to trade one objective off

against another. An example might be the move to conduct business electronically, supporting customers to conduct business in that way and to create the necessary systems to support the electronic operation

- a *business cycle* programme where multiple projects are co-ordinated within cyclic, financial or resource constraints – for example, projects which are funded from a single budget allocation but that actually have little else in common
- a strategy or *infrastructure programme* where overall progress is dependent on investment in un-related projects to agreed standards or in activities that move forward the organisation's goals
- a *research and development* programme where many independent project initiatives are assessed and re-focused within certain guidelines of interim and long-term goals
- innovative *partnership* arrangements where organisations collaborate to establish the sponsorship and management of a programme. The partnerships may involve two or more organisations from the same industry or market sector, or the partnership may bring together organisations from different industries where the respective competencies are seen to provide mutual benefits. Partnerships of this sort may be seen as an alternative to buy-outs, mergers, or take-overs by enabling all parties to remain in their own businesses but with each organisation now able to benefit from increased opportunity, market reach, alignment or integration of service, improved customer service, or any combination of these.

Programme Management techniques can also be of great value in the 'super-project' context where a large, complex but single-objective project is run as a programme – for example, a major construction project. The various activities and different disciplines of these 'super-projects' require similar approaches to co-ordination and management as other programmes.

Despite the broad range of examples and types of programme discussed above, there are common themes that indicate perhaps three main scenarios. These are not necessarily mutually exclusive. Table 3 outlines the three scenarios.

Table 3: *Programme scenarios*	Programme scenario	Description
	Single vision programme	where projects are selected or adopted to become part of achieving a strategic vision. The costs, benefits and risks (the Business Case) associated with the programme are all managed within the sponsoring organisation although third party providers may be contracted to deliver specific services on the programme

Unconnected projects	management of a largely unconnected range of projects as a programme where the portfolio of projects is related to financial, functional or resource management needs
Multi-organisation partnerships	where each party provides some form of input to achieving a shared vision and where each participating organisation has its own business objectives which it hopes to achieve alongside the shared vision. In this situation, it can be complex to develop the Business Case (for example, who should develop it? how do you achieve commitment from all parties?) It is also difficult to identify the stakeholders, how they will be involved and the incentives that will secure their commitment. Multi-organisation partnerships are becoming increasingly common

1.8 Who should read this guide?

This guide is intended primarily for those who are involved in directing and managing programmes – Programme Managers, Programme Directors, Business Change Managers, and Programme Support Office personnel (see *Programme Management organisation*, chapter 3, for the definitions of these roles).

This guide will also be of interest to:
- members of the executive management board of organisations who are responsible for commissioning programmes and appointing Programme Directors
- business managers who are responsible for the realisation of the benefits identified within a programme
- people involved in the direction, steering or management of projects that are part of a programme
- people who are members of project teams or who make audit or assurance contributions to projects, if their projects are to be implemented within a programme
- those responsible for strategic planning and as a precursor for programmes
- management consultancies and services providers, who may be employed to support or work within a programme.

two

OVERVIEW OF PROGRAMME MANAGEMENT

2.1 Introduction

Programme Management is a structured framework for defining and implementing change within an organisation. The framework covers organisation, processes, outputs and ways of thinking that focus on delivering new capabilities and realising benefits from these capabilities. The new capabilities may be services, service improvements, working practices or products that are developed and delivered by projects. The programme selects or commissions projects, providing the overall co-ordination, control and integration of the projects' delivery.

Programme Management includes the process of managing benefits from their initial identification and definition through to the eventual realisation and achievement of measurable improvements. The driver for a programme is the ongoing viability and relevance of the programme's Business Case and the justification of benefit against costs.

2.2 The Programme Management environment

Figure 2 shows a typical environment for Programme Management. Business strategies are shaped by influences from both the internal and the external business environment. Programmes then need to be established to implement those strategies and also to implement further initiatives along the way. Even as programmes are in the process of implementing improvements to their target business operations, they may need to respond to changes in the strategies or to accommodate new initiatives.

Programmes, in turn, initiate or adopt the projects that are needed to create new products or service capabilities, or to effect changes in the business operations, until, finally, the vision for the future is achieved and the full benefits of the programme can be realised. A key element of managing a programme is to formulate a clear model of the improved business operations (this can be thought of as a Blueprint for those operations), which must be maintained and managed throughout the course of the programme.

Programme Management requires the understanding and management of:
- *Benefits*
  The identification and definition of benefits to the organisation and the management and measurement processes required to ensure that they are realised
- *Risks and issues*
  The recognition and management of risks that, if they happen, will adversely affect the operation of the programme and its outputs. Issues are current problems and challenges that require management intervention to enable the programme to remain on track

Figure 2:
The Programme
Management environment

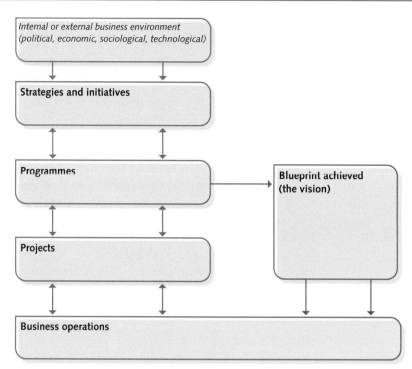

- *Finance*
  The financial management of all programme and project activities
- *Stakeholders*
  The identification of stakeholders, together with detailed analysis of their individual interests and involvement in the programme and its outcomes
- *Communication*
  The ongoing communication that establishes two-way information flows between the programme and its stakeholders
- *Quality*
  The process of building quality into the management of the programme and its deliverables
- *Configuration management*
  The control of documentation and key deliverables for the programme
- *Process*
  The management processes that identify and define the programme; establish the programme's infrastructure and plans; manage the projects and their delivery; and realise the benefits.

2.3 The Vision Statement

The Vision Statement is a customer-facing definition of what to expect from the transformed organisation, its service levels, cost, etc. The Vision Statement is used to communicate the 'end-goal' of the programme to the stakeholders. The new capability might be to deliver a particular service, to perform the same service but in a more efficient way, or simply to be better than the competition.

2.4 The Blueprint

The Blueprint defines the structure and composition of the changed organisation that, after delivery, should demonstrate the capabilities expressed in the Vision Statement. The Blueprint is a detailed description of what the organisation looks like in terms of its business processes, people, information systems and facilities and its data. It is used to maintain the focus of the programme on the delivery of the new capability.

2.5 Programme Management processes

The processes of Programme Management are:

- *Identifying a programme*
  To structure and formalise the programme based on the strategic initiatives of the sponsoring organisations
- *Defining a programme*
  To develop a complete definition of the programme such that the funding requirements can be committed
- *Establishing a programme*
  To set up the programme environment in terms of personnel, working practices and standards
- *Managing the portfolio*
  To manage the Project Portfolio such that the required benefits are delivered
- *Delivering benefits*
  To manage the benefits realisation process and to provide a transition to the new ways of working
- *Closing a programme*
  To formally close down the programme and confirm delivery of the Blueprint and Vision Statement.

2.6 Programme Management organisation

A Programme Management organisation structure, with clearly defined roles and responsibilities, is required in order to establish and define a programme and then effectively manage its implementation, delivery and realisation of benefits. The ultimate responsibility and accountability for the programme lies with the Programme Director who is drawn from the senior executives of the sponsoring organisation for the programme.

The Programme Manager is responsible for the setting up and running of the programme and co-ordinating the projects within it such that the required project outputs are delivered efficiently and effectively. The Business Change Manager is responsible for the benefits management process and ensuring the organisation is ready to take on the new capabilities delivered by the projects. The Business Change Manager ensures that the organisation is able to realise the benefits from the new capabilities.

There is a fundamental difference between the delivery of the new capability and actually realising measurable benefits as a result of implementing that capability. This difference is reflected in the complementary roles of Programme Manager and Business Change Manager.

2.7 **Programmes and projects**

Programme Management provides an umbrella under which several projects can be co-ordinated. This does not replace Project Management; rather, it is a supplementary framework (see Figure 3). Programmes need to be underpinned by a controlled environment of effective Project Management and reporting disciplines for all projects within the programme.

Figure 3:
Programmes and projects

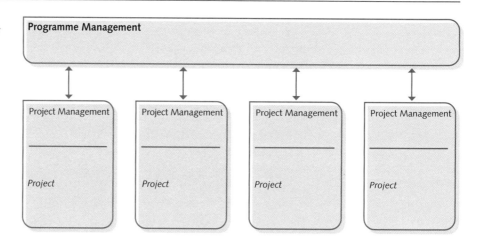

2.8 **Differences between programmes and projects**

A project has a definite start and finish point, with the aim of the delivery of an output that may be a product, service or specific outcome. A programme has a vision of the 'end-state', but no clearly defined path to get there. Benefits accrue at the end of a project, after the output has been delivered. In contrast, a programme will co-ordinate the delivery from a set of projects such that benefits can be realised within the timescales of the programme as well as afterwards. A programme is likely to include some projects that do not directly produce benefits but are nonetheless essential to delivering the overall programme benefits. Relative timescales are also a way of differentiating between a project and a programme. Projects typically have a shorter timeframe for completion than programmes.

The ways in which projects and programmes are managed also demonstrates that a project is different from a programme. Some typical differences between Project Management and Programme Management are shown in Table 4.

Table 4: *Some typical differences between Project Management and Programme Management*	Project Management	Programme Management
	Is an intense and focused activity that is 'driven' by the outputs that are to be delivered	Is a broadly spread activity and is concerned with more broadly defined change objectives
	Includes change control mechanisms but is best suited to objectives that are closely bounded and relatively certain	Is suited to managing large numbers of projects and activities with complex and changing inter-relationships, in an uncertain environment (that is, a larger and more dynamic environment)
	Is about managing the delivery of a product, service or specific outcome	Produces, through synergy, a wider set of benefits than the total of individual project benefits
	Aims to deliver benefits at the end of the project	Is suited to managing the impact of, and the benefits from, the deliverables from a number of component projects and ensuring that there is a smooth and risk-reduced transition into a new business operation
		Delivers benefits both during and after conclusion of the work, having put in place the measurement mechanisms required to demonstrate delivery of the target benefits over time
		Continues until the organisation has achieved its Blueprint, which generally coincides with completion of all the constituent projects. (A programme may of course be stopped earlier if it is no longer viable or relevant)

There are inherent tensions between the pressures on projects to complete to time and budget and the need to achieve the wider goals of the programme. Compromises will inevitably be required as the programme is implemented. These compromises, if they are left to individual project teams, may seriously prejudice attainment of the wider goals and benefits. Programme Management disciplines and structures will help to highlight the need for adjustment as circumstances change enabling conflicts to be recognised early and corrective action put in place.

2.9 Managing a group of projects

A group of projects running within an organisation may not necessarily be aligned to the same goal, or set of goals, or even be interrelated. It is impossible, to justify or align such projects to programme-type objectives, such as the vision of the 'end-state'. However, adopting Programme Management techniques can bring advantages and disadvantages to an otherwise unstructured method of overseeing several projects, as shown in Table 5.

Table 5: *Managing a group of projects – advantages and disadvantages*	Advantages	Disadvantages
	Establishment of common reporting and other standards for all projects provides a better understanding of accountabilities between projects and the central programme management function	There is a risk in expecting a central function to monitor inter-dependencies between projects that share no single vision
	Grouping all project related activities within a business area may free operational business units from the need to manage what can be unfamiliar entities	Where multiple projects are run without a collective goal, overall tracking of progress is impractical
	The purchasing power of several projects can be combined, providing greater buying leverage and leading to economies of scale when negotiating resources common to a number of projects (for instance, contract staff or IT hardware)	Where multiple projects are run without a collective goal, it is difficult to make rational and objective argument about which projects should receive priority and when. The projects with the most powerful sponsors, project executive and project managers may dominate in competition for resources and priority – which may not be in the organisation's best interests
	Economies of resource utilisation may be achieved through the establishment and use of a common Project Support function Use of a common Project Support function may also enable: • better coordination of activities through establishment and maintenance of a consolidated diary for all projects • avoidance of resource conflicts through better scheduling • better organisational resource planning better support for projects, through improved understanding of the overall project driven demands	Multiple individual projects are less likely to be sponsored and tracked at the highest level of management in the organisation, and may thus not be appropriately aligned to the organisation's strategic goals
	Resource management may be optimised, especially personnel, through the establishment of a 'pooled' approach to resource utilisation.	

THE PRINCIPLES OF
PROGRAMME MANAGEMENT

three

PROGRAMME MANAGEMENT ORGANISATION

3.1 Key management principles

Programme Management organisation brings together key roles, processes and management structures to deliver a programme's desired outcomes. The organisation structure and roles discussed in this chapter provide the basis for effective programme management. The structure, roles and individual responsibilities should be adjusted to reflect the particular circumstances of each programme.

Effective management of a programme requires:

- empowered decision making
- leadership at a sufficiently senior level to:
  - ensure resources are committed
  - gain real commitment to the programme's vision and Blueprint
  - influence the stakeholders
  - ensure the programme's priorities are balanced with those of the ongoing business operations
- active management of:
  - the programme's finances
  - the change in business operations
  - realising the business benefits targeted by the programme
  - the co-ordination of the projects within the programme
  - conflicting demand for resources
  - the integration of programme deliverables with the design of new or existing systems and processes
  - the transition to new operational services
- a flexible and responsive management structure that enables well-informed, top-down decision making
- communication in a vocabulary understood by all
- integrity and collaboration amongst all involved in the programme.

However competent the personnel and however effective procedures in both Programme Management and Project Management, some things will go wrong, the unexpected will arise and major unplanned changes may be called for. These major changes can be achieved only through informed decision making and a flexible management regime – that is, people and procedures. Programme Management is most effective when issues are freely debated and risks are openly evaluated. This requires a style and culture of management, as well as working practices and procedures, that encourages the flow of information between the constituent projects and the programme level. Every opportunity to advance the programme towards its goals should be welcomed and converted into constructive progress for the programme. To help create such an open, flexible and well informed regime, there should be active management of changes within the programme and well defined procedures for change control, conflict escalation, issue management and management of risk.

3.2 Programme sponsorship

Every programme requires sponsorship from the most senior executives of the organisation or group of organisations committed to the programme. Programme sponsorship involves the endorsement and underwriting of the overall Business Case for the programme. Sponsorship also includes senior management commitment to supporting the changes introduced by the programme and the utilisation of the new capabilities delivered by the programme to ensure that the required benefits are achieved. Where two or more organisations are working in partnership on a programme, establishing the relative contributions from each can be complex. For example, one organisation may be providing the majority of the funding for the purchase of assets such as new buildings, another may be providing the staffing and systems resources. The group representing the sponsors for a programme is called the Sponsoring Group.

3.3 Programme Management roles

The application of a Programme Management regime should not automatically impose the need for additional management resources. The Programme Management roles and responsibilities described in this guide should be seen as 'logical roles' that, for a small programme, may simply be expansions of existing responsibilities. For a major programme, however, the work and responsibilities of these roles will be very considerable and the costs of a fully constituted Programme Management structure with full-time participation as well as additional support would be justified. In all cases, however, it is essential that the key responsibilities are clearly defined and understood by all personnel involved.

The roles needed to manage a programme should not be passive roles to monitor and review events; rather, they should be proactive and action-oriented roles, with responsibility and accountability to match. There are three primary roles for managing a programme:

- *Programme Director*
  Overall leadership and ultimate accountability for the programme
- *Programme Manager*
  Responsibility for day-to-day management of the programme, its risks, issues, conflicts, priorities, communications, and ensuring delivery of the new capabilities
- *Business Change Manager*
  Responsibility for realising the benefits through the integration of the new capabilities into the business operations.

Figure 4 shows programme and project roles. These primary roles focus on specific aspects of the programme and they should not be merged together. Depending on the size, complexity and significance of the programme, some of the responsibilities

Figure 4:
Programme and
project roles

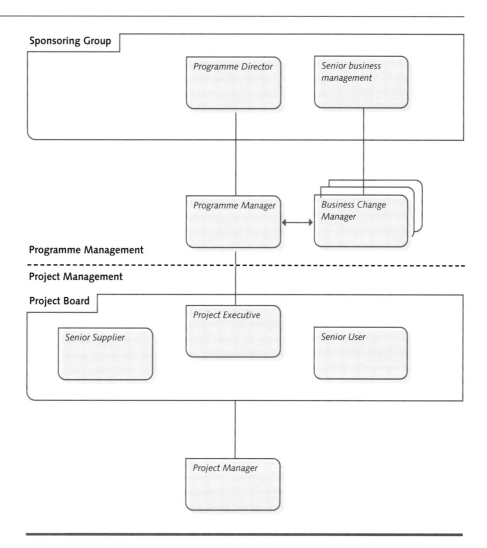

of these primary roles may be assigned to further specific roles, such as Risk Manager, Quality Manager, Communications Manager.

Staff management

Resources and services required by the programme may be provided by in-house service groups or by third parties. The programme will be led by senior business managers and other planners from within the organisation; however, providers of support and infrastructure services should be involved in the setting up of a programme organisation to ensure that any impact on their plans and operations is well understood. External management advice and consultancy support may also be helpful to facilitate the organisation of a programme, but it is critical that top management control is maintained by the sponsoring organisation. At both the programme and project level, the organisation structure for the programme should be designed to support contractual relationships with either in-house service providers or with third parties. The overall authority for the programme, however, must remain within business management control.

Programmes tend to be in existence for a considerable time, during which members of the programme organisation may be involved on a full or part-time basis. Given the duration of many programmes, potentially over many years, adequate support for staff is vital to their success.

Some Programme Management roles may require full-time staffing throughout the life of the programme. The effort required for other roles might be consistent at less than full time contribution, or might fluctuate dependent on what is happening in the programme. Invariably, the programme organisation will combine people who are working full time on the programme with others who divide their time between the programme and other duties. Personnel may be seconded to the programme for long periods, and may be involved to such an extent that it is not practical for their 'parent' organisation to attend to their career and personnel needs. The programme may have to take account of the career needs of those people who are separated from their normal organisational structures.

3.4 The Programme Director

Overall responsibility, leadership and authority for the programme is assigned to the role of Programme Director. The individual who fulfils this role is typically drawn from the Sponsoring Group, the group of senior managers responsible for the areas of the business(es) targeted by the programme. The appointed Programme Director may only be involved part-time on the programme but must be visibly and consistently the driving force throughout the programme. The Programme Director is ultimately accountable for the success of the programme and the individual appointed must be empowered to direct the programme effectively.

The Programme Director has personal accountability for realising the benefits and is responsible for:
- 'owning' the vision for the programme
- securing the investment required to run the programme and realise the benefits
- managing the interfaces and communication with the programme's stakeholders (see *Stakeholder management*, chapter 6)
- ensuring the linkages are maintained between the programme and the organisation's strategic direction
- ensuring that the organisation and staff are managed carefully through the process of change from the old operational business environment to the new, that the results are reviewed, and that adjustments are made, if necessary, to achieve the results as planned
- ensuring that the aims of the programme and its projects continue to be aligned with evolving business needs
- commissioning reviews (the Programme Benefits Reviews) that formally assess the achievements of the projects and the benefits realised from the investment

- overall control of the programme implementation, with personal responsibility for the programme's achievement; this should be an important measure of that individual's performance
- establishing the programme, securing sufficient resources and monitoring progress.

The Programme Director is ultimately responsible for enabling the organisation to exploit the new environment, meeting the new business needs and delivering new levels of performance, benefit, service delivery, value or market share, as appropriate to the particular programme.

It may be necessary to establish a Programme Board in situations where a single Programme Director cannot be sufficiently empowered. The Programme Board members will then collectively take on the role of Programme Director.

The Programme Director's skills and attributes

Successful programmes require strong leadership and decision-making skills. However, different types of programme require different styles of leadership. The Programme Director needs to be able to combine realism with openness and with clarity of expression to communicate the programme's vision effectively. In addition, the Programme Director must have:
- the strength to make decisions that are often strategic in nature
- access to and understanding of the business information necessary to make the right decisions
- access to and stature with key stakeholders
- the ability to communicate the aims and objectives of the programme, and visibly to lead its execution.

3.5 The Programme Manager

The role of Programme Manager is responsible for delivering the new capability through the management of the programme's portfolio of projects, on behalf of the Programme Director. The appointed individual is responsible for:
- managing the programme's budget on behalf of the Programme Director, monitoring the expenditures and costs against delivered and realised benefits as the programme progresses
- planning the programme and monitoring its overall progress, resolving issues and initiating corrective action as appropriate
- facilitating the appointment of individuals to the Project Management teams
- ensuring the delivery of new products or services from the projects is to the appropriate levels of quality, on time and within budget, in accordance with the Programme Plan
- ensuring maximum efficiency in the allocation of common resources and skills within the Project Portfolio
- quality assurance and overall integrity of the programme – focusing inwardly on the internal consistency of the programme; and outwardly on its coherence with

infrastructure planning, interfaces with other programmes and corporate technical and specialist standards

- managing third party contributions to the programme as appropriate
- the communications with all stakeholders
- managing both the dependencies and the interfaces between projects
- management of risks to the programme's successful outcome
- initiating extra activities wherever gaps in the programme are identified
- reporting progress of the programme at regular intervals to the Programme Director.

The Programme Manager ensures the coherence of the programme, and develops and maintains the appropriate environment to support each individual project within it – typically through the Programme Support Office. Support will require systems and procedures to be implemented; it may include the provision of training for those involved with the programme, the Project Executives (Project Boards) and Project Managers.

As the programme is implemented, changes may be suggested that will affect the overall design integrity of an architecture, policy or standard that extends right across the projects in the Portfolio. In other instances, the changes may have an impact outside the programme (for example, a change to the IT infrastructure may affect systems in other business operations). The Programme Manager's responsibilities for overall integrity and quality assurance may be assigned to a separate role such as 'Design Authority', 'Compliance Management Function', 'Strategic Architect' or 'Programme Assurance', typically reporting to the Programme Manager.

Once projects become established, the Programme Manager focuses on monitoring inter-dependencies between projects and changes within the Project Portfolio; the day-to-day Project Management is performed by the designated teams. Throughout the programme, the Programme Manager reassesses whether or not projects continue to meet the programme's objectives and continue to use available funds and resources efficiently. This requires the timely management of exceptions, slippage and issues of priority.

The Programme Manager's skills and attributes

The Programme Manager must have strong leadership and management skills, and may well have a Project Management background. However, the individual appointed must also be capable of understanding the wider objectives of the programme, be able to influence others, and be able to develop and maintain effective working relationships with senior managers, with the Project Executives, and with third party service providers involved in the management and operations of the programme.

The Programme Manager should also have:

- effective interpersonal and communication skills

- the ability to create a sense of community amongst the disparate members of the project teams
- a good knowledge of techniques for planning, monitoring and controlling programmes
- a good knowledge of Project Management approaches – for example, PRINCE2
- a good knowledge of budgeting and resource allocation procedures
- sufficient seniority and credibility to advise project teams on their projects in relation to the programme
- the ability to find ways of solving or pre-empting problems.

3.6 The Business Change Manager

The Business Change Manager role represents the Sponsoring Group's interests in the final outcome of the programme, in terms of measured improvements in business performance. Where the programme affects a wide range of business operations, more than one Business Change Manager may be appointed, each with a specific area of the business to focus on. The individual, or individuals, appointed as Business Change Manager(s) is typically drawn from the relevant business areas and are likely to have ongoing responsibilities within their business areas. If not, they must work closely with the managers of the future business operations in order to ensure that the delivered benefits from the programme are fully realised.

A Business Change Manager's principal responsibilities are to:
- ensure the interests of the Sponsoring Group are met by the programme
- work with the Programme Manager to ensure that the scope of each project covers the necessary aspects required to deliver the products or services that will lead to operational benefits
- assist the Programme Manager to identify the benefits common to two or more projects
- optimise the timing of the release of project deliverables to the business operations
- prepare the affected business areas for the transition to new ways of working and to manage them through the transition process
- establish the mechanisms by which benefits can be delivered and measured
- ensure that maximum improvements are made in the existing and new business operations as groups of projects deliver their products into operational use
- lead all the activities associated with benefits realisation and ensure that continued accrual of benefits can be achieved and measured after the programme has been completed.

As the programme progresses, the Business Change Manager(s) is responsible for monitoring outcomes against what was predicted in the Business Case. At specific points in the programme, defined in the Programme Plan, the Business Change Manager(s) should assess the realisation of benefits and confirm the continuing viability of the programme.

The Business Change Manager's skills and attributes

The Business Change Manager(s) require detailed knowledge of the business environment and direct business experience, and in particular, an understanding of the management structures, politics and culture of the organisation(s) involved in the programme. Business Change Manager(s) need management skills to co-ordinate programme personnel from different disciplines and with differing viewpoints. They need effective marketing and communication skills to 'sell' the programme vision to staff at all levels of the business operation. Business Change Manager(s) should also have experience and management skills to be able to bring order to complex situations and be able to keep a focus on the programme's objectives.

Knowledge of certain management techniques may also be useful, for example:
- business change techniques, such as business process re-engineering
- benefits identification and management techniques.

3.7 Programme and project roles

The Programme Director is typically appointed from within the Sponsoring Group and will therefore be in a position to regularly consult with and seek input from other members at a similar level within the organisation. The Business Change Manager(s), typically appointed from existing operational management, reports to specific members of this group.

Figure 4 shows the relationship between the Business Change Manager(s) and the Programme Manager. There is a fundamental difference between the delivery of a new capability and actually realising measurable benefits as a result of implementing that capability. This difference is reflected in the complementary roles of Programme Manager and Business Change Manager. The Programme Manager is responsible for delivering the capability, the Business Change Manager is responsible for realising the resultant benefits. Individuals appointed to each role must be able to work well together, in close partnership and as an effective team, in order to fully understand and exploit the opportunities for change.

Figure 5 shows how the team of Programme Manager and Business Change Manager(s) can 'double up' on project level responsibilities. The Programme Manager may be able to take on specific project responsibilities as the Project Executive for one or more projects within the programme. However, this extra responsibility and the associated activities (such as attending Project Board meetings) must not be allowed to jeopardise the individual's ability to remain focused on the programme as a whole. In a similar way and with similar caution, Business Change Manager(s) are often well placed to take on the responsibilities of Senior Users, or possibly Project Executives, on Project Boards for the projects within their business areas.

3.8 Tailoring the organisation structure

All programmes should have a clear line of sponsorship, authority, and management. The organisation structure shown in Figures 4 and 5 may need to be adapted to suit different interests and needs on a particular programme. For instance, where more

Figure 5:
Linked roles

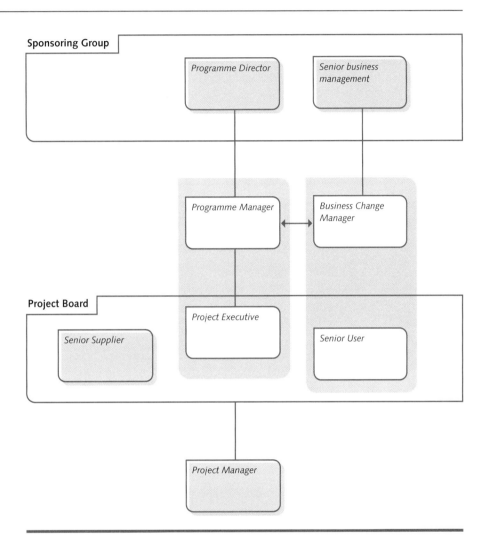

than one organisation is collaborating together to establish a programme, the Programme Director may be the chairperson of a steering committee involving key senior members of the participating organisations.

On very large complex programmes, the management capacity will need to be scaled up to cope with the challenges of managing the programme. The primary roles may need to be supported by the specific allocation of activities to other individuals, such as Communications Manager, Risk Manager and Finance Manager.

Each programme should be directed and managed with the appropriate level of management resources to enable clear direction setting and effective management of ongoing progress, but without incurring excessive management overheads for the programme.

3.9 Programme assurance

The purpose of programme assurance is to assure the Sponsoring Group and other key stakeholders in the programme that the programme is being managed appropriately and that the objectives for the programme are, or will be, met satisfactorily. Programme assurance is part of the role of each member of the Programme Management team. Considerations for establishing the specific responsibilities for programme assurance include the following:

- what is to be assured? The management processes, the maintenance of key programme documents, for example
- what skills and experience is required to be able to undertake the required assurance?
- how will assurance be undertaken for the programme as a whole and for the projects within it?
- what outputs will be required from the assurance function?
- how will the assurance function maintain an awareness of the changing environment in which the programme is operating?

3.10 The Programme Support Office

For most programmes, a Programme Support Office should be established to collect, co-ordinate, analyse and distribute management information about the programme. This management information derives both from the programme's management processes and, in summarised form, from the management processes of the projects. The Programme Support Office may only provide this type of information management and control function. However, depending on the skills and availability of appropriate resources, the Programme Support Office may also be able to provide training and consultancy advice to the programme and its projects, or it may be able to provide facilitation for certain Programme Management activities, such as identification of potential benefits, or resolving prioritisation problems.

An IT system and support tools are generally required to provide support for the information management of programmes. In many respects, the system will be similar to a project control system, but it should be capable of facilitating the resource and cost scheduling across multiple projects and potentially across several organisations.

A Programme Support Office can serve both the programme and the individual projects within the programme (see Figure 6). Its role would then be to act as a focus for all project reporting and control activities as well as to provide the management information and document control for the programme. Activities include the following:

- holding master copies of all programme documentation
- assisting the Programme Manager with budget control for the programme
- establishing and maintaining the index to an electronic library of programme information
- maintaining status reports on all projects in the programme
- analysing interfaces and critical dependencies between projects and recommending appropriate actions to the Programme Manager

Figure 6:
Programme and
Project Support

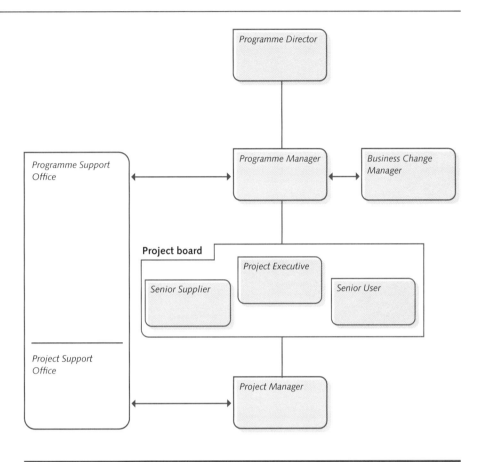

- establishing consistent practices and standards of project planning, reporting and control
- providing advice and support to Project Managers in preparing the appropriate progress reporting information
- registering issues for subsequent investigation and resolution using the Issues Log
- monitoring items identified as requiring action, prompting timely actions and reporting on whether required actions have been carried out
- maintaining the list of stakeholders and their interests
- analysing risks and maintaining and updating the Risk Log for the programme
- generating all necessary quality management documentation
- maintaining and updating programme documentation
- producing and distributing of reports from Programme Benefit Reviews
- maintaining and updating the Programme Plan
- configuration management of all programme documentation and deliverables
- maintaining and monitoring the programme's change control procedures.

four

PROGRAMME PLANNING

4.1 Introduction

The principal objective of planning a programme is to organise the work in a way that accomplishes the programme's objectives and delivers the benefits. One of the major challenges in running a programme is to reconcile project objectives and accountability with the overall programme goals and programme level consistency and control. Successful Programme Management requires the careful delineation of project boundaries with a rigorous identification and active management of inter-project dependencies. The projects will inevitably experience the day-to-day problems associated with keeping on track. Delays to one project will affect other projects within the programme, thus making programme planning and monitoring a complex activity.

4.2 Inputs to programme planning

Programme planning is not simply project planning on a larger scale. Planning a programme requires the integration of various strategies so that the Programme Plan reflects not only the schedule of projects within the Project Portfolio, but also the way the programme is to manage quality, risk, communications, and benefits. The strategies for the approaches to each of these provide a major input to developing the Programme Plan, including:

- what level of detail the Programme Plan should go to, and what tools will be used to monitor and maintain the Plan
- what the programme and project level activities will be, and when they will be done, to meet the quality requirements for the programme
- what information will be distributed to whom and when as part of achieving the required communications for the programme
- what risk management activities will be required and when they will happen
- how and when the benefits are going to be tracked and monitored during the programme.

The drivers for the programme may relate to specific benefits to be achieved by a given deadline, or they may relate to external dependencies over which the organisation has no control, such as the launch date for a new currency. The drivers should be recognised and used to bound the overall timescales within which the programme must operate.

4.3 The Programme Plan

The Programme Plan is a key control document for the programme. It enables the Programme Manager, on behalf of the Programme Director, to ensure that a planned and controlled environment is established and maintained throughout the life of the programme. The Programme Plan provides the basis for tracking the impact of each project on the programme's overall goals, benefits, risks and costs. It also enables the

Table 6: *Contents of a Programme Plan*	**Programme Plan content**	**Description**
	Project information	the list of projects (the Project Portfolio) and their target timescales. A Dependency Network showing the optimum sequencing of the projects and their dependencies on each other
	Costs	a schedule of costs associated with each project and when they will be incurred
	Benefits planning	a schedule of all the benefits to be delivered by the projects and when they will be achieved
	Risks	a summary of the identified risks that, if they happen, will affect the Programme Plan. The programme's Risk Log contains the detailed information on all the risks to the programme
	Shared resources	a profile of the resources required by the projects that are shared across more than one project within the portfolio. The profile should show the expected utilisation by each project of the shared resources within time periods. This profile is used to monitor, understand and react to any shifts in resource utilisation by one project that could affect others. Resources that are dedicated to individual projects need not be monitored at the programme level as they fall under the responsibility of the individual Project Management teams
	Programme Schedule	a schedule of the Project Portfolio showing review points where decisions can or need to be taken, where progress can be assessed and any changes considered that will update the Programme Plan. Review points may correspond to the closure of projects, or to time-based points such as monthly or quarterly reviews or regular management meetings. The schedule should also include details of communications activities and quality review work for the programme

Programme Manager to monitor the dynamics of the inter-relationships between each project and to act when a delay in any one project might jeopardise the work of others.

Developing and maintaining the Programme Plan requires the ongoing co-ordination of all the Project Plans. The focus for programme planning is on the inter-dependencies between the projects and any dependencies on external factors outside the control of the programme. The Programme Plan is a 'living' entity, providing a definitive and up-to-date picture of the programme from which reports can be drawn to analyse and publicise the current status of the programme. The Programme Plan should contain the information shown in Table 6.

4.4 The planning process

Programme planning is a continuous process. The Programme Plan is formulated, reviewed and refined throughout the programme lifecycle. The key steps in this cycle include:

- the definition of programme tranches – the first of these emerging as the programme is defined (see *Defining a Programme*, chapter 13) and others following as the programme progresses through the tranches (see *Managing the Project Portfolio*, chapter 15)
- the increasing refinement of individual Project Plans as each project proceeds through its stages
- exception situations on the projects (either external influences or internal variances) that will cause a re-appraisal and review of the Programme Plan.

Tranches

On major programmes with a large number of projects, it is useful to group the projects into *tranches*. A tranche is a specific grouping of one or more projects within the Project Portfolio. The tranches are generally structured around distinct step changes in organisational capability such as increasing competencies or improving the organisation's infrastructure. It is rare for a programme to achieve its objectives through a single tranche of projects. As each tranche is completed it brings a distinct benefit or set of benefits to the organisation. Grouping projects in this way requires consideration of the schedule of benefits and the Dependency Network in order to identify the optimum definition of tranches.

Delineating projects may be helped by considering the following types of approach:
- *grouping by discipline* – programmes tend to be multi-disciplinary, whereas projects are often seen as single discipline. Projects can be defined and scoped so that each involves a single discipline
- *grouping by location* – a multi-site project is inherently difficult to manage, largely because of the communication overheads between members of the project team and Project Management. Projects may be scoped by grouping together the activities that can be achieved at a single site

- *grouping by deliverables* – projects can be scoped by grouping the required deliverables so that each project is responsible for a single, or closely related set of, deliverables
- *avoiding contention for resources* – any input required by a project is a 'resource' and includes people, time, materials or services. Minimising resource sharing between projects will help prevent 'bottlenecks' occurring.

Delineating projects will require pragmatism. Reducing dependencies is just as important as identifying clearly manageable projects.

Defining and scoping the projects is critical to the programme's eventual success. The objective is to place very clear and direct accountability onto the Project Boards, whilst avoiding a spaghetti-like tangle of inter-dependencies between projects. The advantages of this are:
- to avoid overlaps between projects and hence promote clear accountability
- to keep the interfaces between projects to a minimum so that central co-ordination of the Project Portfolio is made easier.

4.5 Shared resources

The planning process will identify a number of resources that need to be shared between projects. Typical examples are:
- *staff* – where people are involved with more than one project within the programme
- *infrastructure or facilities* – for example, where office space may need to be shared
- *information* – where multiple projects update a shared repository of data
- *third party services* – where several projects make use of a common service provider.

Shared resources represent a set of dependencies between projects as well as representing an asset that needs to be used efficiently. Shared resources need to be co-ordinated at the programme level.

4.6 The Dependency Network

The programme's deliverables and their target delivery dates are identified during the development of the Blueprint (see *Defining a Programme*, chapter 13). Each of these deliverables (or products) should be defined with the following information:
- description
- title of project responsible for delivery
- dependencies to other projects and/or products
- dependencies on other projects and/or products.

The Dependency Network shows all inputs to and outputs from the projects, treating each project as a 'black box'. It enables the Programme Manager to schedule the projects and to analyse the impact of any potential slippages. The Dependency Network should also identify the 'float' available for each dependency – that is, the delay that can be tolerated before a slippage by one project in turn delays another. A stylised example of a Dependency Network is shown in Figure 7.

Figure 7:
Example Dependency
Network

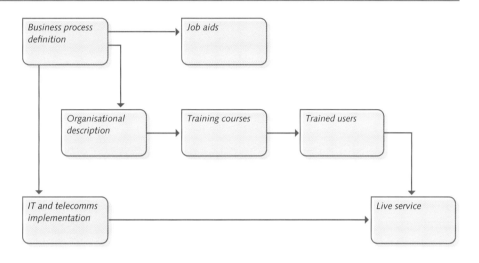

4.7 Programme scheduling

The Dependency Network provides the basis for the Programme Schedule by indicating the relative timescales of each project. The grouping of projects into tranches is represented in the Programme Schedule. Figure 8 shows an example Programme Schedule. The end of each tranche provides a strategic review point for the programme in order to assess achievements to date and confirm any necessary realignment or changes to the programme's strategies.

4.8 Project Briefs

The Project Portfolio includes new projects that are to be commissioned by the programme, and existing projects that will need to be 'adopted' into the Portfolio. For new projects, the programme should provide as much detail as possible about the project – such as, what it is to deliver, how it fits into the overall Portfolio, budgets for resources, the target timescales, any dependencies on other projects and risks related to the project. This information forms the Project Brief that is used by the Project Board and Project Manager to get the project off to a controlled start. (In PRINCE2, the Project Brief is the basis for the development of the Project Initiation Document or PID). The Project Brief is a key document providing the direction and scope of the project. It forms the 'contract' between Project Management and Programme Management.

The Project Brief should contain the following information:
- background and status of the programme and the project
- project definition including objectives, scope, deliverables and/or outcomes, any exclusions, constraints, and interfaces

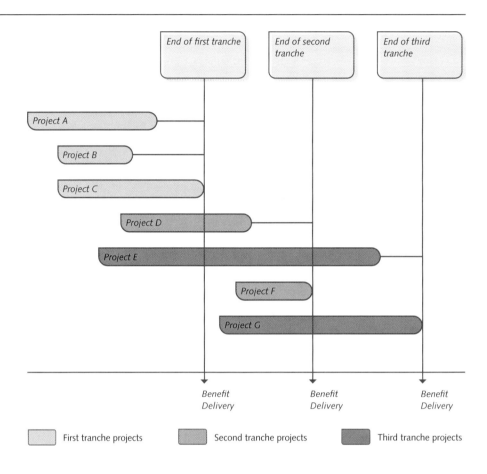

Figure 8:
Example Programme
Schedule

- an outline Business Case for the project, indicating how it supports the programme and links to the benefits
- estimated resources and costs
- quality expectations
- project sponsor responsible for the project
- acceptance criteria for the project
- any known risks affecting the project.

A programme will not always commission new projects. The projects that deliver
parts of the Blueprint may already be running within the organisation; in this case the
programme needs to adopt these projects into the Portfolio. To adopt a project, its
status should be assessed to determine its 'fit' to the Blueprint. The project may need
to be re-directed to align more closely to the Blueprint. Any such changes to the
project scope, plans, or deliverables should be managed under formal change control
procedures. The Project Management team will need to be briefed on the way the

project is to progress following its adoption into the programme. Once the project is aligned to the Blueprint, it can be added to the programme's Project Portfolio and tracked as part of the overall monitoring of the Programme Plan.

4.9 Monitoring and maintaining the Programme Plan

As the programme progresses, project managers for the projects within the Portfolio should submit regular reports (in PRINCE2, these are the project's Highlight Reports) summarising their actual and projected delivery of products or outcomes. These reports should include specific details on delivery dates, typically in the form of 'best case' and 'worst case'.

By monitoring the Programme Plan closely, the Programme Manager will be alerted to any inter-project dependencies that are becoming critical in terms of delivery dates, resource utilisation, or costs and benefits. The Programme Plan should be publicised regularly to ensure all affected and interested parties are kept fully informed and able to provide feedback as appropriate.

five

BENEFITS MANAGEMENT

5.1 What is benefits management?

> **Definition of benefits management**
>
> Benefits management is the activity of identifying, optimising and tracking the expected benefits from business change to ensure that they are achieved.

The fundamental purpose of a programme is to transform the organisation in some way, to do things differently, or to do different things. The programme's Vision Statement describes the desired outcome of this transformation. Benefits management provides the programme with a target and a means of monitoring achievement against that target on a regular basis. The information provided by benefits management indicates whether the programme is a success. Benefits management is a core activity and a continuous management process running throughout the programme. After completion of the programme, the benefits management process will continue because some benefits, (possibly the majority of them), may not come 'on stream' until well after the programme has been completed. The focus of benefits management is on the actual realisation of benefits; care should be taken not to shift this focus to the delivery of new capability.

Benefits management covers:
- defining the business benefits expected from the programme. The nature of these benefits must be clearly understood and accepted by all those responsible for them and involved in delivering them
- understanding the off-set of benefits against the costs of achieving them
- planning how the benefits will be achieved and measured
- allocating responsibility for successful delivery of benefits
- monitoring the achievement of benefits as systematically as the tracking of costs.

Figure 9 represents the process cycle for benefits management.

Programmes are typically significant and highly visible to the organisations that they change and to the organisations upon which they have an effect. Throughout the programme, it is important to continually monitor the degree to which the programme benefits remain valid from the perception of the stakeholders.

5.2 Realising benefits

To ensure that benefits are eventually realised, they must be positively managed from the start. The successful realisation of benefits requires active monitoring of

Figure 9:
Benefits management
process

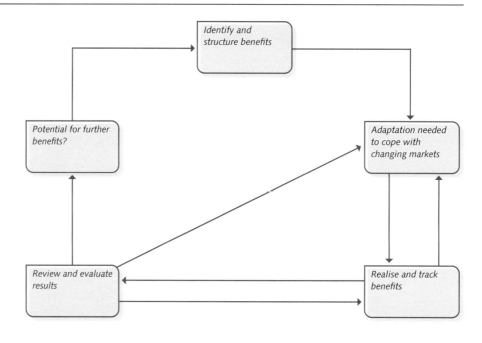

programme and project deliveries. It also requires a degree of 'post delivery support' to help the business operations take full advantage of the new capability or service delivered. Responsibility for realisation of benefits lies with the business operations. The programme will deliver the new capability, service, or working practices, and will ensure that the business operations are ready to implement them. Realising the measurable effects of the change means building the new capability into the operations so that it becomes 'business as usual'.

5.3 Identifying benefits

The benefits required by the organisation should be identified and defined as early as possible at the beginning of a programme. In many situations, the organisation's business strategy will identify the types of benefit that should be achieved. The definition of the programme will then refine these into measurable benefits to be achieved by the programme. Benefits may be considered in a number of different categories, as shown in Table 7.

Benefits can accrue in a number of ways and can be expressed in various financial and non-financial terms. For instance, the emergency services might perceive a reduction in the time to treat a victim or resolve an incident to be a critical business benefit. Alternatively, the social services might regard the reduction in the number of children on the 'at risk' register as a measure of success.

Table 7: *Categories of benefit*	Category of benefit	Description
	Mandatory	benefits that allow an organisation to fulfil policy objectives or satisfy legal requirements, where the organisation has no choice but to comply
	Quality of service	benefits to customers, such as quicker response to queries, providing information required in a way the customer wants
	Internal management benefits	benefits that are internal to the organisation, such as improving the quality of decision making or management productivity
	Increased productivity	benefits that allow an organisation to do the same job with less resource, allowing reduction in cost, or to do more. This may also be termed 'efficiency'
	More motivated workforce	the benefits of a better motivated workforce may lead to a number of other benefits such as flexibility or increased productivity
	Risk reduction	benefits that enable an organisation to be better prepared for the future by, for example, not closing off courses of action, or by providing new ones
	Flexibility	benefits that allow an organisation to respond to change without incurring additional expenditure
	Economy	benefits that reduce costs whilst maintaining quality (often referred to as cost reduction)
	Revenue enhancement and acceleration	benefits that enable increased revenue, or the same revenue level in a shorter timeframe
	Strategic fit	benefits that enable the desired benefits of other initiatives to be realised

5.4 Dis-benefits

As well as considering the expected benefits from the programme, dis-benefits should also be identified, measured and tracked in order to minimise their impact. A dis-benefit is an unfavourable outcome and may occur because of:

- a bad implementation of new processes, such as inadequate training for users of a new system resulting in increased delays rather than reductions
- inherent dis-benefits which no amount of planning or forethought can eliminate completely, such as the introduction of a new system which transfers decision-making from the central office to individual business units. There is an advantage (of greater flexibility and responsiveness to the customer) to the organisation as a whole, but for the individual units taking on more tasks, it is a dis-benefit.

5.5 Quantifying benefits

In order to assess whether a benefit has made a measurable impact, it is useful to consider whether the benefit can be quantified or not. For example:

- can it be quantified and valued? (a direct financial benefit)
- can it be quantified, but difficult or impossible to value? (a direct non-financial benefit)
- can it be identified but not easily be quantified?

Some benefits will be perceptions and impressions rather than specific tangible outcomes. These intangible benefits may be more difficult to quantify and measure but it is important to develop ways to recognise when a perception, for example, has been improved. Questionnaires and interviews are often used to gauge intangible improvements. Figure 10 gives some examples of direct and indirect benefits.

Quantifying benefits involves considering the inevitable trade-off between the cost of achieving the benefit against the value to the organisation of having that benefit. Figure 11 represents the concept of net benefits, where the cost of a benefit is tracked against its value.

5.6 Benefit Profiles

The benefits (and dis-benefits) identified need to be defined so that the programme can monitor and track their progress. The definition of a benefit is called the Benefit Profile. As the programme is set up and established, the benefits information should be documented into Benefit Profiles. The Benefit Profiles should be agreed with the managers of the business areas where the benefits will actually be realised. The Benefit Profiles can then be managed and controlled by the Business Change Manager(s) with the same degree of rigour as costs, for both are of primary importance to the success of the programme.

The Benefit Profiles should detail:

- the description of each benefit or dis-benefit
- how the measurement or test of the benefit achieved will be carried out
- projected changes from the current business processes and operations
- inter-dependencies with other benefits

- key performance indicators in the business operations now and for the future, and current or baseline performance levels
- explicit linkages, wherever possible, between projects and benefits
- dependencies on risks and other programmes or projects
- financial valuations of the benefit where possible
- when the benefit is expected to occur and over what period of time will realisation take place.

Figure 10:
Examples of direct and indirect benefits

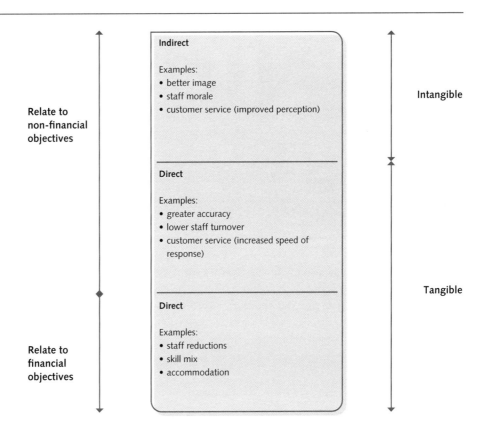

The definition of the benefits must pass four critical tests:
1. *description* – what precisely is this benefit?
2. *observation* – what differences should be noticeable between the pre- and post-programme business operation in a Programme Benefits Review or audit?
3. *attribution* – where in the future business operations does the benefit arise?
4. *measurement* – how will the benefit and the achievement of the benefit be measured?

Figure 11:
Net benefits

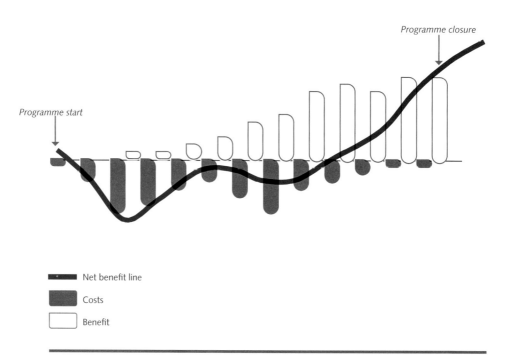

Throughout the running of a programme, potential improvements in the target business operations should be reassessed and the Benefits Profiles reviewed and adjusted as necessary. Benefits may be realised from the changes made by individual projects or by a group of projects. Some projects may not deliver benefits in their own right, but require the same monitoring and tracking because they may be providing pre-requisites for other projects that will deliver the benefit.

5.7 **The Benefits Management Strategy**

The Benefits Management Strategy is perhaps the most important piece of programme information. It should be continually reviewed and maintained throughout the programme. The Benefits Management Strategy defines how the achievement of benefits will be actively managed during the programme. Figure 12 shows a series of questions that may be useful in developing the Benefits Management Strategy.

Providing answers to the questions presented in Figure 12, the Benefits Management Strategy should include:
- an overall benefit statement relating to the programme's Blueprint
- the Benefit Profiles (including any dis-benefits identified)
- how expectations will be managed through the ups and downs of running the programme and benefits realisation
- formal review points when an assessment of the benefits achieved will be carried out (Programme Benefit Reviews)

- how changes to the Blueprint and business operations will be controlled as benefits are realised.

5.8 Programme Benefit Reviews

Programme Benefit Reviews may be scheduled at any point during the programme as well as after the programme has completed. The objectives of the Programme Benefit Reviews are to:

- inform those managing the programme of progress in benefits delivery and realisation, and to help identify any further potential for benefits
- assess the performance of the changed business operations against their original performance levels
- assess the level of benefits achieved against the planned Benefits Profiles
- review the effectiveness of the way benefits management is being handled, so that improved methods can be developed and lessons learned for the future.

Programme Benefit Reviews may be scheduled to include the individual project reviews (in PRINCE2 these are called Post Project Reviews) for projects that have been completed within the programme. There is often a tendency to be over optimistic when defining the expected benefits from a programme. Unfortunately, over-optimistic expectations can inhibit the buy-in and commitment from staff and cause the Programme Benefit Reviews to become 'witch hunts'.

The following questions may help structure a Programme Benefit Review:

- which planned benefits have been achieved? If they have been achieved, were the targets correct or should they have been increased?
- which planned benefits have not been achieved? Why were they not achieved? Can remedial action be taken to achieve them or has the opportunity been lost?
- is there a pattern to the success/failure that can be used to inform other realisation plans?
- were the assumptions on which the realisation of the benefits was based correct? If not, what effect did this have on the realisation process?
- were there any unexpected benefits that have resulted? If so, can they now be planned and maximised further?
- have the dis-benefits been managed and minimised?
- were there any unexpected dis-benefits? If so, how can these be managed and minimised?
- are there any further potential benefits?
- do the measures applied appear to be the correct ones? Do they need changing or refining? Was the process of data collection to establish the measures effective?

The findings of each of the Programme Benefit Reviews should be disseminated to the rest of the programme.

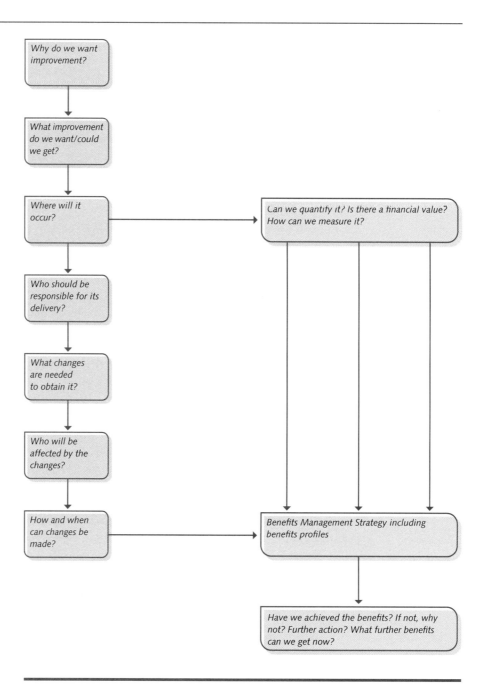

Figure 12:
Developing the Benefits
Management Strategy

5.9 Responsibilities for benefits management

Benefits management responsibilities may be divided into four areas, as shown in Table 8.

Table 8: Responsibilities for benefits management

Benefits management process	Responsibility
Identifying and defining	carried out by the Business Change Manager(s) and business area managers and agreed with the Programme Director
Planning, monitoring and tracking	carried out by the Programme Support Office. The Programme Manager is responsible for tracking and co-ordinating the progress of projects to ensure they deliver outputs to the business such that the benefits can be realised
Realisation	carried out by the specific business managers in the affected areas who work with the programme's Business Change Manager(s). The Business Change Managers are also responsible for preparing the organisation for the new capability to be delivered
Assessment	review against defined performance improvement targets. Usually carried out by individuals who have good knowledge of the target business areas but are not directly involved in the programme itself

Responsibility for the actual realisation of benefits will fall to the business managers in the relevant areas; however, they will need to be fully involved in the identification and definition process in order to accept this responsibility. The achievement of benefits should be assessed independently from the process of delivery (that is the programme); however, stakeholders and business managers will need to be interviewed as part of this assessment.

six

STAKEHOLDER MANAGEMENT

6.1 Identifying stakeholders

Over the life of the programme, there will be many individuals and groups who have an interest in, or who are involved in, or who are affected by, its activities and outcomes. These interested parties are the stakeholders and include the people managing and working within the programme, together with people or organisations directly or indirectly contributing to or affected by the programme. Programmes inevitably affect a number of stakeholder groups. During the life of the programme, stakeholders may come and go, depending on the activities of the programme. However, key stakeholders, such as the programme's sponsors, will remain constant throughout the programme.

Some stakeholders will be able to participate in the programme from an advisory or assurance perspective; others will be a key group for assessing the realisation of the programme's benefits; others will have an audit perspective. There may be individuals or groups who will be worse off as a result of the programme and who are therefore potential 'blockers' to the progress of the programme. Both the positive and negative viewpoints should be considered as part of stakeholder management.

Stakeholders may be identified from the following:
- owners or shareholders, executive management, operational management and staff of the organisation(s) sponsoring the programme
- owners or shareholders, executive management, operational management and staff of the organisation(s) affected by the programme
- customers or consumers who will be affected by the programme's outcome
- owners or shareholders, executive management, operational management and staff of the organisation(s) supplying goods or services to the programme or its constituent projects
- owners or shareholders, executive management, operational management and staff of the organisation(s) supplying goods or services to organisation(s) affected by the programme (either positively or negatively)
- internal and/or external audit
- security personnel
- Trade Unions
- regulatory bodies
- the wider community in which the affected organisation(s) exist
- Project Management teams established to deliver the projects within the programme
- the Programme Management team.

6.2 Stakeholder analysis

Each of the stakeholders will have a specific interest area, such as financial, technical, regulatory, personnel management. When identifying the stakeholders for a programme, it is important to recognise their specific interest areas in order to ensure that their expectations can be managed effectively. Information dissemination and two-way communications are critical for managing expectations effectively.

A Stakeholder Map is a useful tool for identifying and planning the necessary communications process for a programme. A Stakeholder Map lists each of the stakeholders against their particular interest area in the programme.

6.3 Stakeholder communications

Programme success relies on co-operative contributions and support from all involved. However, achieving success will inevitably involve trade-offs between one set of interests against another. Co-operation and support will only be forthcoming if the stakeholders in the programme have (and maintain) a good understanding about the programme and its progress, and are able to feel that their perspectives are respected and considered. Programme communications should be directed both outward, to gain support from the community whose operations will be affected by the changes it will bring about, and inward, to those establishing and implementing the programme. Communication channels should be established so that stakeholders' expectations of the programme can be managed and maintained throughout the programme's life.

The objectives of the communications process are to:
- keep awareness and commitment high
- maintain consistent messages within and outside the programme
- ensure that expectations do not become out of line with what will be delivered.

Successful communications will be judged on their ability to meet these objectives and generally promote a feeling of common ownership. The communications process will itself identify specific difficulties or obstacles that will need to be addressed. A continuing and two-way approach to communications is essential between the programme and its stakeholders.

Open and informal internal communications help to build the identity and commitment of the personnel involved with managing the programme and its projects. Effective dialogue between all members of the Programme Management team also assists the decision-making processes. Reliable, accurate and up-to-date information is essential to help balance the issues and priorities for the programme from a top-down perspective.

6.4 The Communications Strategy

A Communications Strategy for a programme defines how communications will be established and managed during the running of the programme. Developing the Strategy will involve:

- confirming the identity of the relevant stakeholders and their needs
- identifying the information to be communicated, both outward from the programme and inward to the programme from the stakeholders
- selecting the appropriate way(s) of communicating to each (for example briefings newsletters, presentations), and the required frequencies
- developing a Communications Plan to implement the Strategy
- defining the associated costs and including these in the overall Financial Plan for the programme.

Communication is central to any change process – the greater the amount of change, the greater the need for clear communication about the reasons, the benefits, the plans and proposed effects of that change. It is important, therefore, that the Communications Strategy should be defined and implemented as early as possible and then adequately maintained throughout the programme.

A key objective is to communicate early successes both to those directly concerned with the business operation, and to other key audiences, especially where rapid progress in realising benefits is required. The aim is to secure commitment and build momentum. Thereafter, effective communications will also facilitate knowledge-transfer across programme staff and into the business operations.

The Communications Strategy should be designed with the following objectives:
- raising awareness of the benefits and impact of the Blueprint
- gaining commitment from staff in the target business area(s) to the changes being introduced – thus ensuring the long term success of the improvements
- keeping all staff in the target business area(s) informed of progress before, during and after implementation or delivery of project outcomes
- demonstrating a commitment to meeting the requirements of those sponsoring the programme
- making communications truly two-way by actively encouraging stakeholders to provide feedback and ensuring they are informed about the use of their feedback to influence the programme
- ensuring all those responsible for projects have a common understanding of the changes involved in the programme
- maximising the benefits obtained from the new business operations.

The Communications Strategy should answer the following questions:
- what are the objectives of communications?
- what are the key messages?
- who are you trying to reach?
- what information will be communicated?
- when will information be disseminated, and what are the relevant timings?
- how much information will be provided, and to what level of detail?

- what mechanisms will be used to disseminate information?
- how will feedback be encouraged, what will be done as a result of feedback?

The answers to these questions may be different for each of the stakeholder groups. Any variations should be identified during the analysis of stakeholders and documented on the Stakeholder Map.

6.5 Achieving successful communication

Successful communications are based on four core elements:
- message clarity, to ensure relevance and recognition
- audience identification (or segmentation) – to target successfully according to requirements
- a system of collection to obtain feedback and assess the effectiveness of the communications process
- a system of delivery to bring the above together.

Messages to be delivered must be consistent. They should be derived from the programme's objectives and be simple, short and few in number. It may be useful to use 'touchstone statements' and/or 'sound-bites or word-bites' as the foundation for more complex communications and then to repeat these throughout the programme. This approach will help individuals to recognise specialised elements within an understandable framework and ensure the organisation is seen to be speaking with 'one voice'.

The implementation of a Communications Strategy inevitably involves various issues, all of which will need to be addressed, for example:
- the scale of cultural and organisational change
- management of expectations over an extended period
- the need for business ownership of the overall programme
- the need for staff buy-in and involvement
- the need for marketing and communications expertise to support the Programme Director
- the requirement for clarity and consistency of messages and benefits.

Failure to address any one of these areas can potentially affect the successful implementation of the programme.

To gain the most from the Communications Strategy, the total audience could be segmented to ensure that the most appropriate communications mechanisms are used for each group. Figure 13 shows some typical groupings.

Each group will have specific needs and requirements that may be best addressed on an individual group basis rather than by general communication. It may also be necessary to tailor communications to meet the particular needs of the target audiences, whilst still maintaining consistency throughout messages.

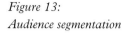

Figure 13:
Audience segmentation

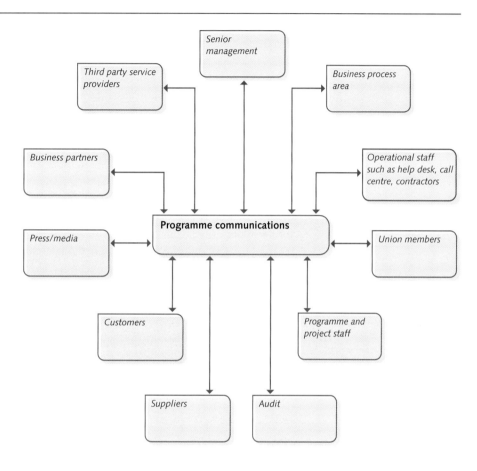

6.6 Communication channels	The channels used to achieve communications may be a mixture of 'participative' approaches, for example seminars or presentations, and 'non-participative', for example, memos or newsletters. The effectiveness of each channel used on the programme should be monitored as the programme progresses. Changes should be made to cater for the evolving requirements of the audiences, as their knowledge increases and demand for information grows. Some of the channel options are summarised below.	
Seminars	Seminars are a powerful medium and can be split into events for business staff and those for programme and project members. The aim of the business staff seminars will be two-fold: to bring staff up-to-date on the progress of the programme (and to allay any fears they may have), and to provide a forum for staff to ask questions of those managing the programme. The benefit of this approach is that it provides those responsible for Programme Management with an opportunity for direct contact with stakeholders and for obtaining first-hand feedback on issues directly affecting them.	

It also helps in projecting consistent messages, themes and policies on the most important issues.

The aim of the programme/project member seminars is to ensure that everyone 'buys in' to the programme and feels part of the overall team. These seminars should be designed to provide a forum for highlighting successes and raising issues. They will serve to further engender the sense of common responsibility and ownership for the task in hand. This has been shown to be a particularly effective means of ensuring that projects run to plan. It will also provide the programme with an informal mechanism within issue management for understanding project issues, or any other issues in a discussion environment rather than on a formal progress reporting basis.

Bulletins

There are two types of bulletins – general, and specific to a stakeholder or audience group. The general bulletins should provide an update on the programme, addressing issues of concern to all staff, such as overall progress or any changes to the programme objectives. The specific bulletins should provide the particular stakeholder(s) with information relating to their own issues. Bulletins may be distributed effectively via intranet home pages or email. However, it is important to make sure that stakeholders have access to email or the home pages, are aware of their existence, and want to visit them. In addition to web pages, it is often useful and more convenient to distribute the bulletins in paper form, such as newsletters, so that people can take them home, or read them on the train.

Site exhibitions

Static displays should be placed at each main site outlining the reason for the programme, the effects it will have on the site, the people and the benefits expected both at a strategic and local level.

Video

Video films, when targeted appropriately, are an extremely cost-effective means of communication and could be used to provide updates on progress and for 'selling' the key programme messages.

CDs

CDs presenting a range of information about the programme allow individuals to find information relevant to their particular interests. Frequently asked questions (FAQs) and answers can be easily formulated using this medium.

Briefings

Regular briefings can help keep stakeholders updated on progress.

Hints and tips

A regular 'Hints and tips' sheet could be produced with the aim of engendering more widespread use of outputs and of any training courses and materials that are available. 'Hints and tips' should be produced in-house to a professional standard.

seven

ISSUE MANAGEMENT
AND RISK MANAGEMENT

7.1 Issue management

An 'issue' is a major problem that is preventing the achievement of the programme's objectives in some way and cannot be resolved using normal management action. Programme issues are normally raised if they lie outside established problem/incident reporting mechanisms, such as the issue management processes at the project level. Managing programme issues takes place within the wider context of management processes.

Figure 14:
Issue management

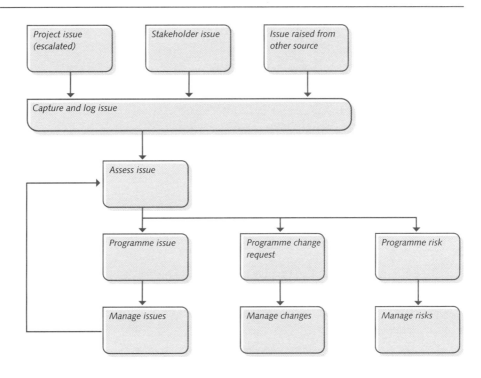

All programme issues will need to be logged and tracked to ensure their effective resolution. It is useful to establish an Issues Log that the Programme Manager can use to capture and maintain information about the issues raised and their current status. Once logged, the issues can then be assessed and categorised in order to direct the appropriate management actions. Figure 14 represents the processes involved in issue management.

7.2 Programme risks

Programmes are established to achieve significant change through the co-ordinated execution of multiple projects. Programmes typically involve communications from numerous parts of the sponsoring organisation(s), together with contributions from service providers, suppliers and other third party organisations. The programme environment is complex and dynamic. At any point in a programme's life there will be events or situations that may adversely affect the direction of the programme, the delivery of its outputs or achievement of its benefits. These are the programme's risks.

Successful Programme Management requires constant vigilance and appropriate and timely action against the realisation of programme risks. Programme risks may be related to a wide variety of causes including the management of business change, programme and project change or technical aspects of the programme. Managing and monitoring these risks should be built into the programme's decision-making processes.

7.3 The Risk Management Strategy

The Risk Management Strategy guides the programme to reduce or mitigate risk, to develop alternative courses of action and to communicate both the means of averting risks and the responsibilities for this. The likelihood and the impact of perceived risks may change over time. Some risks may become greater as a result of another unforeseen event occurring, and new risks may need to be identified as implementation progresses. The Risk Management Strategy should, therefore, be kept under review and updated as risks change.

The Risk Management Strategy defines how the programme will approach the following:
- the identification of all risks to the successful outcome of the programme and its projects
- the maintenance and updating of a Risk Log
- the assessment of risks and possible countermeasures
- details of responsibilities and processes for risk monitoring and control
- detailed plans for managing the risks
- other roles and responsibilities, for example risk owners.

7.4 Identification of risks

Annex A gives a list of questions that may be useful to ask when considering the risks that threaten the success of the programme. The list is for guidance only and is not intended to be exhaustive. It provides a starting point for the identification of programme risks, but should be expanded with the risks that are specific to each particular programme environment.

Strategic-level risks

At the strategic level, consideration must be given to the consequences of failing to realise the opportunities for business benefit. At this level, there are also drivers (such as political pressures, emerging technologies and new initiatives) arising while the programme is under way, which may alter the programme's scope and lead to changes in direction – a source of further risk to the programme.

Serious risks lie in any failure to ensure a common understanding among the sponsors and other stakeholders of the programme's business change objectives and requirements. Such failure will, of course, affect the direction and chances of success of the entire programme. Where two or more programmes are being implemented in an organisation, there are likely to be risks that need to be considered when the programmes are scoped and planned. Changes at the strategic level, such as new initiatives that the organisation must respond to quickly, can affect these programme inter-dependencies and the associated risks.

Programme-level risks

A major area of risk to the programme is where project inter-dependencies change, giving rise to new sources of risk. The achievement of the programme's benefits may be frustrated if such risks are not managed. Other risks to the programme may arise if the underlying assumptions of the programme's Business Case change, potentially making the Business Case invalid (due to market changes or competition, for example).

Project-level risks

Much of the focus of the management of risk within programmes comes at the project level. Some project risks may be identified before the projects are underway, for example, when the programme is being set up. When project teams analyse risks, they may gain clearer insight into risks affecting the programme, requiring a revision of the programme's risks. Further risks may be identified due to non-availability of skills and resources that will affect the project's capability to deliver its products or services. Programme Management does require that project level risk management is integrated to the risk management processes at the programme level.

Operational-level risks

As projects deliver their outputs of products and services, the transition to new ways of working and new systems can lead to further sources of risk. For example,from the hand-over process, from the need to maintain 'business as usual' (for more details on Business Continuity Management, see Further Information), as well as the integrity of the systems, infrastructure and support services.

7.5 The Risk Log

As each new risk is identified it should be added to the programme's Risk Log. The Risk Log brings together all the information about the known programme risks and provides a basis for prioritisation, action, control and reporting related to programme risks. Programme risks will typically have different timescales for when they might materialise and affect the programme. Some risks will be predicted to be further away in time than others, and so attention can be focussed on the more immediate ones. The proximity of each risk should be included in the Risk Log. An example Risk Log is shown in Table 9.

Table 9: *Example Risk Log*	*Risk Id*	a unique reference for each risk identified. This reference should be reflected in project level Risk Logs when the risk could impact the programme as well as the project
	Risk description	a description of the risk to the programme and which projects are likely to have an impact on the risk (either increasing its likelihood, or reducing it)
	Programme impact	description of the impact on the programme should the risk materialise
	Proximity	the estimation of timescale for when the risk might materialise. The accuracy of this estimation increases as the point in time approaches. The scale should provide for continuous and equal time windows that will align easily with the programme's risk management processes. For example, if the programme has a planned duration of 30 months and the Programme Management team has agreed to meet every 3 months, then the proximity scale could sensibly use 3 month increments
	Probability	the probability of realisation of the risk. This could be a mathematical calculation, or a simpler High, Medium, Low classification
	Severity	the degree to which the interests of the programme would be harmed by the realisation of the risk. Categories for severity might be Critical (that is, adverse affect on the benefits such that continuation of the programme is unacceptable), Major, Significant, and Minor
	Risk owner	the Programme Manager has overall responsibility for managing programme risks, however it may be useful to assign an individual as the *risk owner* such that the risk can be monitored in detail and appropriate actions can be closely managed
	Countermeasures	actions which either reduce the probability of the risk being realised or reduce the effects of the risk that has been or will be realised
	Current status	the current status of the risk itself and any actions relating to the management of the risk

The Risk Logs created and maintained at the project level within a programme may need to be integrated together to form one single Risk Log for the entire programme. However, this may result in a very large document that is difficult to manage effectively. Interfacing the project level risks with the programme should be considered carefully, to prevent risks not being escalated to the appropriate level and effort being wasted in unnecessary bureaucracy and double-handling.

7.6 Responsibility for managing risks

Risk management is the responsibility of the Programme Manager. However, on complex programmes it is advisable to allocate this specific responsibility to a Risk Manager who has specialist expertise in managing risk.

eight
QUALITY MANAGEMENT

8.1 Introduction

Quality management is a continuous process throughout the life of the programme and should be achieved as an integral part of the day-to-day activities on the programme. The objectives of quality management are to:

- ensure that the outputs produced on behalf of the programme are 'fit for purpose' and produced in accordance with their relevant specifications
- learn lessons from experiences gained within and outside the programme, and incorporate improvements wherever appropriate
- balance the need to keep everyone informed through the wide circulation of programme documents with the need to make best use of people's time by selective targeting of document circulation
- provide the Programme Management roles that are assigned to individuals with detailed responsibilities, including relevant responsibilities for quality
- define and implement procedures for ensuring quality in the programme's delivery of the Blueprint, such as quality reviews, inspections, testing
- establish a programme assurance function.

8.2 Responsibility for quality

The Programme Manager is responsible for all aspects of quality on the programme. On large programmes it may be useful to assign the activities of quality management to a specific role of Quality Manager or as part of a Design Authority role.

The Business Change Manager(s) is responsible for ensuring quality is engineered into the final business operations, to ensure that quality performance will deliver maximum benefits from the changes brought about by the programme.

8.3 The Quality Management Strategy

The strategy for building quality into the programme should reflect any corporate process control standards and product control standards that are applied within the organisation. The Quality Management Strategy should include:

- definition of the organisational responsibilities for quality management
- definition of the information to be used and produced by quality management
- definition of any software support tools to be used to support quality management, for example change control tools
- definition of the resources required for quality management
- definition of quality assurance, review and control processes for the programme including:
  - what will be subject to quality assurance, review and control
  - who will undertake quality assurance, review and control activities
  - what the triggers are for these activities (time, events, risk)
  - what actions will be taken depending on the results of quality checks.

8.4 Quality management and contracts

Quality management should be included within the contracts management processes on a programme where formal contracts are placed.

Contractual requirements need to be adequately defined and documented so that:

- third party providers have the capability to meet the requirements
- any changes to the base requirements over time are formally agreed and documented.

Contract review activities, interfaces and communications should be co-ordinated with other programme activities.

nine

CONFIGURATION MANAGEMENT

9.1 Introduction

Configuration management is the process of keeping related information complete and up-to-date by continuous monitoring, control and recording of changes.

Key sets of information that are fundamental to the monitoring and control of a programme include the Vision Statement, the Blueprint, and the Programme Plan. Information about the programme is collected, presented and distributed to various parties throughout the programme in the form of documents or sets of documents in electronic and/or paper form. As the programme progresses, this information is refined, updated, amended and extended. The effective management of this information so that it remains up-to-date and aligned with what is really happening 'on the ground' is a vital part of managing programmes.

A 'configuration' is a combination of things that together make up a recognised unit. In the context of a programme, the Blueprint consists of information about the organisation, its people, processes, tools, and systems. As the programme delivers change to the organisation, people, processes, tools and systems, the Blueprint will need to be updated to reflect that change. This updating continues throughout the programme as the projects within the Portfolio deliver their respective outcomes or deliverables. The Blueprint is a configuration which must be formally managed as its constituent parts develop and change. Configuration management ensures that the complete Blueprint is always cohesive and consistent.

In addition, the Blueprint itself is a constituent part of another set of information, the combination of Vision Statement, Business Case, and Programme Plan. This combination of information must be maintained so that it is mutually consistent and cohesive; it also requires configuration management.

9.2 Configuration management processes

There are five basic processes involved in configuration management:
- deciding what will be subject to configuration management for the programme and identifying the constituent parts
- planning how configuration management will be achieved
- identifying when a constituent part of a 'configuration' will be agreed and 'frozen' so that future changes to it are only made with appropriate levels of agreement and approval
- the recording and reporting of all current and historical information concerned with each 'configuration'
- a series of reviews or audits to ensure there is conformity between the documented 'configuration' and the actual business environment to which that 'configuration' is referring.

9.3 Level of detail

Deciding on the level of detail for each 'configuration' and its constituent parts depends on the nature of the programme and its deliverables. For example, configuration management may be applied to individual products delivered by the projects, or to groups of these products that together form a recognisable whole. Selecting too low a level of detail will result in unnecessary administrative overheads and frustration from projects as they attempt to deliver their products.

9.4 Change control

Change control is the process of managing and controlling the changes to programme and project deliverables, documents and other tangible products. In a programme context, change control should be applied to the key sets of information about the programme, such as the Blueprint and the Programme Plan. The process may also be applied to products during their development stages on a project. In this case, change control would be applied at the project level.

Defining the procedures for change control on a programme requires consideration of the following:
- maintaining a central log of potential changes
- establishing a mechanism for prioritising the potential changes
- carrying out formal impact assessments of the potential changes against the programme's Business Case, Programme Plan, Project Portfolio, Blueprint, etc
- assessing the impact of the change on the risks to the programme, or to the expected benefits
- re-evaluating the priority status
- decision processes for deciding which changes to accommodate
- updating the log with the decision and maintaining an audit trail
- implementing the approved changes appropriately and communicating the outcome to those affected.

9.5 Escalating changes to the programme level

Each project team within the Portfolio is responsible for its own project's change control. However, certain changes will have an impact outside the project, either on other projects within the Portfolio or on the Programme Plan. The programme should specify the tolerance levels for any such changes at the project level so that only those changes that matter to the programme are escalated to the programme level. It is important for all the project teams to have a common understanding of the change control process for the programme. The aim is to balance the need to communicate changes to all interested parties with the overhead of too much administration.

ten

AUDIT

10.1 Overview

Programmes are typically required to demonstrate that the management processes employed are effective and appropriate and that the particular needs of stakeholders are being – or are likely to be – met. Audit is a generic activity, not one confined solely to the audit of financial accounts, and is often used to assess the management and conduct of a programme. Audit involves examination of the activities of a programme with the aim of determining the extent to which they conform to accepted criteria. The criteria may be internal standards and procedures or external codes of practice, accounting standards, contract conditions or statutory requirements.

Programme auditors should be able to provide the programme with their particular information needs and be able to assist the Programme Manager to build in any specific audit requirements to the procedures and plans for the programme.

10.2 Audit requirements

Typical audit requirements that should be built into the Programme Management processes include consideration of the following:

- which stakeholders are likely to require independent assurance, for what purpose and how frequently?
- what records and audit trails will be necessary to satisfy these requirements? The requirements may fall under categories of management decisions on policy, strategy and tactical approaches, transaction records, process control records and records of system use. The Programme Support Office will be responsible for administration of all information about the programme. It may be necessary to appoint a specific role for this task on large programmes
- how long will it be necessary to retain such information? Contract documents, for example, may extend over a considerable period of time and may be required well after completion of the programme in the event of disputes
- how are records to be recovered for audit scrutiny? Information management of programme documentation will require careful consideration about how to catalogue, file, store and retrieve information
- where programme records only exist in electronic form, how will their authenticity be demonstrated? It should not be assumed that electronic, as opposed to paper, records will form acceptable evidence to auditors
- is the Programme Management framework and processes adequately documented? Internal audit, in particular, will typically be concerned with providing senior management with assurance that the approach is functioning effectively. However, comprehensive and useable documentation about how the programme is being managed also provides a source of reference for all personnel involved in the programme.

PROGRAMME MANAGEMENT PROCESSES

eleven

PROGRAMME MANAGEMENT PROCESSES: OVERVIEW

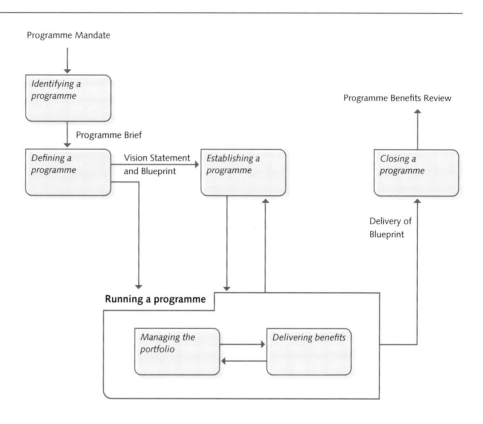

Figure 15:
Programme
Management processes

11.1 Introduction

Figure 15 shows the processes for Programme Management. The first process is triggered by a Programme Mandate that provides the high level requirements of the programme. The Mandate is provided by the programme's sponsors (the Sponsoring Group) who identify and appoint the Programme Director. From the Mandate, the end-goals and approach that the programme will adopt is developed in the form of the programme's Vision Statement and Blueprint. Before a programme should begin establishing the management and support processes, a complete definition of the programme is documented. This programme documentation includes a detailed description of the required projects (the Project Portfolio), how the programme will operate, who is responsible for what, and how and when the programme will deliver the required benefits.

Running a programme involves a continuous cycle of ongoing management of the Project Portfolio and delivery and realisation of benefits until the Blueprint is delivered and the capabilities required to deliver the vision are achieved. Throughout the running of a programme, there should be a continual assessment of 'are we still on track?', 'is the Business Case for this programme still relevant?', 'do we need to change anything to re-align the programme?'.

Programme closure is the formal end-point for the programme, although further Benefit Reviews may be required to assess the achievement of benefits resulting from the final implementations of new capabilities and the delivery of a changed organisation.

11.2 Programme information

Information about the programme and how it is progressing is captured and maintained in a series of documents. The documents are created and maintained throughout the Programme Management processes. The creation and subsequent updating and reviewing of these documents is summarised in Figure 16.

Figure 16:
Matrix of programme information and programme management processes

	Identifying a programme	Defining a programme	Establishing a programme	Managing the portfolio	Delivering benefits	Closing a programme
Programme Mandate	CO					
Programme Brief	CR	RV				
Vision Statement	OC	RF			RV	RV
Blueprint		CR		UP	UP	RV
Benefit Profiles		CR		UP	UP	RV
Benefits Management Strategy and Plan		CR		UP	UP	RV
Communications Strategy and Plan		CR		UP	UP	RV
Financial Plan		CR		UP		RV
Programme Organisation Structure		CR		RV		RV
Quality Management Strategy		CR		RV		RV
Risk Log		CR		UP		RV
Risk Management Strategy		CR		RV		RV
Stakeholder Map		CR		RV		RV
Programme Plan		CR		UP	UP	RV
Project Portfolio		CR		UP		
Business Case		CR		RV	RV	RV
Issues log			CR	UP		RV
Programme policies and procedures			CR	RV		RV
Programme Support Office functions			CR	RV		RV
Programme Benefits Reviews					CR	CR

Abbreviations:

CO confirmed
CR created
OC outline created
RF refined
RV reviewed
UP updated

twelve
IDENTIFYING A PROGRAMME

12.1 Purpose

The purpose of 'Identifying a Programme' is to take the Programme Mandate and to structure and formalise the ideas and concepts into a Programme Brief such that:

- the programme can be identified in terms of what it is being setup to achieve and what the desired benefits are going to be for the organisation(s) involved
- management decisions can be made on whether the programme is justified and whether a commitment should be made to proceed to the next process of 'Defining a Programme'.

'Identifying a Programme' is typically a short process, perhaps taking only a few weeks to complete.

12.2 Activities
The Programme Mandate

The strategic issues facing an organisation will drive the initial scoping of a programme: the programme takes on a range of activities and projects designed to address part, or all, of one or more of these strategic issues. The commitment to begin planning a programme is called the Programme Mandate. The Mandate defines the overall objectives for the programme and positions the programme within the organisation's corporate mission, goals, strategies and other initiatives. The Mandate may be a formal, documented output from the organisation's business strategy. However, it may not exist as a single, cohesive document. In this case, the concepts and objectives of the programme will need to be drawn together using facilitated workshops, interviews and discussions with key members of the organisation's executive and senior management teams.

The Programme Mandate should be a short, but clear, management level statement containing the following information:

- what the programme is intended to deliver in terms of new services and/or operational capability
- how the organisation(s) involved will be improved as a result of delivering the new services/capability
- how the programme fits into the corporate mission and goals and any other initiatives that are already underway or will be underway during the lifetime of the programme.

The Mandate represents the high level business requirements for the programme.

Programme sponsorship

A programme requires top level sponsorship in order to gain, and maintain, the necessary commitment to the expenditure, resources, timescales, and impact of change that will be involved. Senior executives from the organisation form the programme's Sponsoring Group. The Sponsoring Group represents those who have a major strategic interest in the programme and who will be its key stakeholders. Providing the Programme Mandate is the responsibility of the Sponsoring Group.

Appoint the Programme Director

The Programme Director is the 'figurehead' for the programme and has ultimate responsibility for its successful outcome. The Programme Director should be appointed as soon as possible to provide leadership, direction and a focal point for the programme, particularly during the initial planning discussions. The programme will be a major interest for the Sponsoring Group and ideally the Programme Director should be appointed from within this Group.

Produce the Programme Brief

The Programme Brief is the first main deliverable of the programme. It provides the basis for a formal management decision: 'should we proceed with this programme?'. The Programme Brief is prepared from the initial information provided in the Programme Mandate and with significant input from the Sponsoring Group and other relevant senior managers from the organisation(s) who will be involved in the programme. The Programme Director is responsible for preparing the Programme Brief and may require the support of a small team to assist with the work. The Programme Brief should contain the information shown in Table 10.

Table 10: Content of the Programme Brief	**Contents**	**Description**
	Vision Statement	the Vision Statement describes the capability the organisation seeks from changes to the business and/or its operations. Delivery of this capability is the end-goal of the programme. The Vision Statement will be developed further during 'Defining a Programme'. At this point, the Statement is in outline only
	Benefits	an outline description of the type of benefits to be derived from the new capability, when they are likely to be achieved, and how they will be measured. The list of benefits will require some prioritisation to ensure that they occur at an optimum time, accepting that some 'early wins' are often the best way to engender confidence in the programme. Where the programme involves multiple organisations (for instance, one organisation providing sponsorship and funding, another providing resources and skills) the benefits will need to be attributed to or shared across the different

organisations. It is often necessary to consider 'dis-benefits' (where one of the parties may be worse off as a result of the programme) alongside the benefits in order to present a complete and realistic 'picture' of the programme's outcome

Risks and Issues

an explanation of the risks to the programme that can be recognised at this point in time, any current issues that may affect the programme, and any known constraints, assumptions or conflicts that may potentially affect the programme. It is important to be able to balance the desired benefits arising from the programme against the risks and issues that may prevent the benefits from being fully realised

Estimates of costs, timescales and effort

as much detail as possible should be included on the estimated costs, timescales and effort required to set up, manage and run the programme through to delivery and realisation of the benefits in order to give a sound basis for the Business Case for the programme. Programmes tend to be major 'spenders' so it is important to outline the budget requirements, the levels of expenditure that are likely to be incurred and when. The overall timescale for the programme may be relatively long, perhaps two to five years. An outline plan for the programme should cover the list of candidate projects or activities required, and should indicate any other initiatives or programmes that will be underway at the same time. The effort required by the programme will not be known in detail at this point; however, it is important to provide an estimate of the expected resource requirements

---

Terms of reference for 'Defining a programme'

'Defining a Programme' involves the detailed planning and definition of all aspects of the programme. Terms of Reference for this work should be produced, together with a plan for the amount of resources required and the estimated duration.

Gain approval to proceed

The Programme Brief, and the Terms of Reference and plan for 'Defining a Programme', must be formally endorsed and approved by the Sponsoring Group to confirm their understanding of, and overall commitment to, the programme's vision, its expected benefits, risks, issues, timescales, resources and costs.

12.3 Inputs, outputs and decisions

There may be insufficient justification for the programme - for example, the risks and costs may outweigh the potential benefits. The Sponsoring Group may decide to stop the programme at this point, or perhaps decide to pursue further investigation and analysis of other options and alternatives. Table 11 shows the inputs, outputs and decisions associated with 'Identifying a Programme'.

Table 11:
Inputs, outputs and decisions

Item	Type	Notes
Programme Mandate	Input	The trigger for 'Identifying a Programme' that defines the overall objectives for the programme
Programme Brief	Output	Provides the basis for deciding whether the programme is justified
Terms of Reference and plan for 'Defining a Programme'	Output	Description of the work needed to develop a detailed definition of the programme
Appointment of Programme Director	Output	Appointed from within the Sponsoring Group
Approval to proceed or stop	Decision	Formal commitment from the Sponsoring Group to proceed into 'Defining a Programme', or stop, or consider another course of action

12.4 Responsibilities

Table 12 shows the responsibilities for 'Identifying a Programme'.

Table 12:
Responsibilities

Role	Responsibility
Programme Director	Responsible for developing the Programme Brief and Terms of Reference for work on programme definition. May require the support of a small team.
Sponsoring Group	Provide the Programme Mandate. Responsible for giving formal commitment and approval to proceed with the programme

thirteen

DEFINING A PROGRAMME

13.1 Purpose

A programme is a major undertaking for most organisations. Inevitably it will mean significant funding and change to the organisation(s) involved. The activities of 'Defining a Programme' provide the detailed information that establishes the definition of the new capabilities and the way they are going to be delivered. Details of the way the programme will be managed and run, what changes will be implemented within the organisation, what benefits will be delivered and when, and how much it will cost are also defined. The total set of information about the programme is the Programme Definition. The programme's Sponsoring Group must give their approval for the Programme Definition before the programme proceeds. This approval will be conditional on whether the programme presents a sound basis for the investment.

13.2 Activities

Establish a team to define the programme

The Programme Director usually requires the support of a small team to help develop the various strategies and plans for the programme. The Terms of Reference produced in 'Identifying a Programme' should be used to select and appoint the team to develop the formal definition of the programme. The team should have the appropriate skills, knowledge and experience to fully understand the objectives of the programme and be able to develop the definitions and strategies for benefits, risks, quality, communications, business processes, organisation structures, plans, costs, performance levels, and logistics for the programme. Members of the team may subsequently fulfil formal roles defined in the programme's organisation structure. In particular, the Programme Manager may be appointed at this point.

Develop the Vision Statement

The outline Vision Statement developed in the Programme Brief should be further refined to cover:
- a detailed description of the future business capability
- details of the operational measures for future costs, performance and service levels that will be achieved.

The Vision Statement is a business focused definition of what to expect from the transformed organisation, its service levels, cost, etc. The Vision Statement is used to communicate the 'end-goal' of the programme to the stakeholders. The new capability might be to deliver a particular service, to perform the same service but in a more efficient way, or simply to be better than the competition. The following examples illustrate the business-led emphasis that should underpin the programme:
- to manufacture widgets at a cost that is consistently in the lowest quartile of the national widget cost scale
- to deliver HR services to departments in a way that reduces their ongoing recruitment costs by x% per head year on year

Develop the programme's Blueprint

The Blueprint defines the structure and composition of the changed organisation that, after delivery, should exhibit the capabilities expressed in the Vision Statement. The Blueprint is a detailed description of what the organisation looks like in terms of its business processes, people, information systems and facilities, and data. It is used to maintain the focus of the programme on the delivery of the new capability. The Blueprint is rarely capable of development in a single pass. The 'end-state' described in the Vision Statement will typically be reached through progressive refinements (these may become the programme's tranches; see *Programme planning,* chapter 4), to the capabilities of the organisation. Detailed business analysis and design may be helpful to fully explore the opportunities and options for the Blueprint. This work may be carried out as a feasibility study or small project in its own right.

The Blueprint is maintained and refined throughout the programme. It should cover the following information:

- business models of the new functions, processes and operations
- organisation structure, staffing levels, roles and skill requirements necessary to support the future business operations
- information systems, tools, equipment, buildings, required for the future business operations
- the data required for the future business operations
- costs, performance and service levels for the support required for the future business operations.

Develop Benefit Profiles

A Benefit Profile defines when a specific benefit can start to be realised following the delivery of a new capability, and the requirements for the business operations in order to actually realise that benefit. The Benefit Profiles provide a planning and control tool for the programme to track progress on the delivery and realisation of the benefits. The list of benefits (and dis-benefits) identified in the Programme Brief should be reviewed against the Vision Statement and Blueprint to identify any further potential benefits and any dependencies there may be between one benefit and another. A Benefit Profile should be developed for each identified benefit (and dis-benefit). To assess the success (or otherwise) of benefit realisation, each benefit will also require a mechanism for measuring the improvement as a result of its realisation. See Annex B for the suggested content of a Benefit Profile.

Design the programme's organisation structure

The organisation structure for managing a programme must enable effective decision-making on the programme and efficient communication flows around the various members of the programme team. The primary roles for managing a programme are discussed in *Programme Management organisation,* chapter 3. The nature and size of the programme will influence the design of an appropriate organisation structure for managing and supporting the programme. This structure will need to operate alongside the existing line or matrix management structures of the organisation(s) involved in the programme. The programme organisation should reflect the management levels appropriate to the visibility and significance of the programme.

Each role on the Programme Organisation Structure should be defined with the specific responsibilities required. The individuals who will take on these roles and responsibilities should be identified. The amount of work required for each role needs to be balanced against the amount of time that the individual assigned to that role is able to contribute to the programme. It may be necessary to procure third party resources for the programme organisation, thus providing more experienced and specialist skills to fulfil some of the roles. It is important to remember that procurement is normally a lengthy and specification-driven process; sufficient time and resources need to be allowed when planning the procurement of third party assistance.

Design the Project Portfolio The Project Portfolio is a list of the projects that together will deliver the capability described in the Blueprint. The Project Portfolio provides the basis for developing the Programme Plan. There may be options for achieving target improvements or changes in business operations, in which case these should be explored in terms of timing, content, risks and benefits. The projects may be existing, ongoing work that will need to be 'adopted' into the programme as part of the Portfolio; alternatively the projects may be new initiatives that will require commissioning by the programme at the appropriate point. Prioritising the projects into the Portfolio is a major task. The effect on staff and the organisation of delaying or bringing forward a project can be significant. An outline schedule showing the estimated relative timescales for the projects should be developed at this point; more detailed project delineation and planning will be required once the programme has been formally approved.

It may not be possible to identify all of the required projects at this point. For example, further analysis may be required after the results of a first set of enabling projects (for instance, to improve communications or increase competencies) have been assessed.

The organisation may have projects outside the scope of the programme, not included in the Project Portfolio, that potentially conflict with the programme's objectives. These should be recognised and the potential conflict with the programme defined so that appropriate action can be taken when the programme is formally approved.

Stakeholder identification and analysis The programme will inevitably affect the working lives of many individuals and groups. Each of these should be identified, together with their particular interest in the programme. It is also important to identify any stakeholders who are likely to be worse off as a result of the programme, as their interests may lie in preventing the programme's successful outcome. The analysis of stakeholders will identify the various information needs and communication flows that should be established as part of programme communications. A Stakeholder Map is a useful way to capture and manage information about a large number of stakeholders. See Annex B for a suggested content of a Stakeholder Map. The members of the project teams within the Project Portfolio should be included as stakeholders in the programme.

Develop the Communications Strategy and Communications Plan for the programme

The Communications Strategy for the programme should cover information flows outward (from the programme) and inward (into the programme). The programme will need input from the various stakeholders to inform and influence the programme during its implementation.

The Communications Plan indicates when, what, how, and with whom, information flows between the programme and its stakeholders will be established and maintained. In addition to information about change and the implications for the programme, there is a wide range of subject material to be communicated in any programme, including information about:
- Programme Management organisation and arrangements
- people, their in-programme and outside-programme activities
- goals and objectives
- policies, strategies, plans
- achievements, challenges, successes, failures.

Define the Benefits Management Strategy and Benefits Plan

The Benefits Management Strategy describes how the programme's benefits will be managed from initial identification and definition through to delivery and realisation. Responsibility for delivering the capability to achieve the benefit rests with the programme and its projects. However, the Business Change Manager, together with the business managers within the target business areas, will be responsible for actually realising the benefit. The full co-operation and support of these business managers during the identification and planning of the benefits is an important criterion for the ultimate success of the programme.

The Benefit Profiles are used to develop an overall Benefits Plan showing how the total set of benefits will be realised during the programme. The Benefits Plan should show the benefits following the delivery of new capability from the projects within the Project Portfolio.

Define the Quality Management Strategy

The Quality Management Strategy defines the approach the programme will take to ensure that quality is built into the programme's processes and the Project Portfolio from the outset. The Strategy should also cover how quality will be assured in the programme's deliverables. The Programme Plan should include when such assurance activities will be undertaken and by whom.

| *Define the Risk Management Strategy and develop the Risk Log* | The Risk Management Strategy defines how risks to the programme will be identified, analysed, monitored, and controlled. The Strategy should also encompass the processes for the management of risks on projects within the Project Portfolio and should also define how any project risks that affect other parts of the programme will be managed and controlled. The programme requires a central Risk Log to assist the risk monitoring and control activities which should be initiated as soon as the Project Portfolio is developed. |

| *Develop the Programme Plan* | Programme planning is an ongoing process throughout the programme. The Programme Plan is a major control document for the programme. The amount of information available and the level of detail required will develop as the programme progresses. At this point, the Programme Plan should contain the following information: |

- the list of projects (the Project Portfolio)
- the costs associated with each project
- the benefits expected (Benefit Profiles and Benefits Plan)
- the risks identified (the Risk Log)
- the resources required to manage, support and provide assurance to the programme
- an overall schedule for the Project Portfolio (in outline).

| *Prepare the programme's Financial Plan* | The initial estimates of costs and expenditure outlined in the Programme Brief need to be fully developed into a detailed Financial Plan for the programme. The Financial Plan provides details of the overall financial management of the programme (including budget information) and how the financial spend on the programme will be managed and controlled, together with a profile of the expected costs and when they will be incurred. An outline contents list for the Financial Plan is given at Annex B. |

| *Develop the programme's Business Case* | The Business Case presents the programme's costs, benefits and risks so that the overall viability of the programme can be assessed and appropriate management decisions made about whether to continue with the programme or not. The level of detail required in the Business Case will depend on the particular programme and its business environment. It is reviewed regularly throughout the programme to confirm the continued relevance and viability of the programme. A suggested contents list for the Business Case is given in Annex B. |

| *Gain approval to proceed* | The Programme Definition requires a formal endorsement from the programme's Sponsoring Group to confirm that it meets their expectations and requirements. The programme's Vision Statement, Blueprint, and Business Case provide the basis for this endorsement. The Programme Plan, the Financial Plan and the strategies for communications, managing benefits, risks and quality may also be required to provide further details. The Sponsoring Group must give their approval to proceed including their commitment to the funding required for the programme. |

13.3 Inputs, outputs and decisions

Table 13 shows the inputs, outputs and decisions required for 'Defining a programme'.

Table 13:
Inputs, outputs and decisions

Item	Type	Notes
Programme Brief	Input	Approved by Sponsoring Group at the end of 'Identifying a Programme'
Programme Definition containing:	Output	
Blueprint		Describes how the new capability will be delivered by the programme
Vision Statement		Provides the 'end-goal' of the programme
Business Case		Presents the costs, risks and benefits of the programme
Benefits Management Strategy		Describes how the benefits will be managed from identification through to delivery
Benefits Plan		Overall schedule for monitoring when benefits are expected to be realised
Benefit Profiles		Control tools for tracking the progress of each benefit and dis-benefit identified
Risk Management Strategy		Defines how risks will identified, assessed and monitored during the programme
Risk Log		Central documentation on all known programme risks
Quality Management Strategy		Defines how the programme will build quality into its deliverables and processes, and how quality will be reviewed and assessed during the programme
Financial Plan		Defines the programme's financial management and expenditure control procedures, budgets, and projected costs

Programme Plan		The major planning and control information about the programme that includes the Project Portfolio
Communications Strategy		Describes how the programme will establish and maintain communication flows with all the stakeholders
Stakeholder Map		A matrix of stakeholders and their specific interests
Communications Plan		Schedule of how the programme will achieve the communication flows required
Programme Organisation Structure		Tailored organisation structure for managing the programme
Approval to proceed or stop	Decision	Formal commitment from the Sponsoring Group to proceed into 'Establishing a Programme', or to stop the programme at this point

13.4 Responsibilities

Table 14 shows the responsibilities associated with 'Defining a Programme'.

Table 14: Responsibilities	Role	Responsibility
	Programme Director	Overall responsibility for directing the work of defining the programme and for providing the interface with the Sponsoring Group and other stakeholders
	Team appointed to define the programme	Assisting the Programme Director to define and document all the information about the programme
	Sponsoring Group	Endorsement and commitment to the programme

fourteen
ESTABLISHING A PROGRAMME

14.1 Purpose

The purpose of 'Establishing a Programme' is to appoint the individuals to the various management and support roles required for the programme and to ensure the procedures, infrastructure and support mechanisms are set-up. Programmes need to co-ordinate and manage large quantities of data. An efficient management and support regime will enable management attention to focus on delivering the Blueprint.

14.2 Activities

Set up the organisation and people-related elements of the programme

The Programme Director should appoint the Programme Manager and ensure the other individuals identified as part of the organisation structure for the programme are appointed. The Programme Support Office is established by appointing the necessary personnel to administer the programme's document management system, provide support for the programme's planning and management processes, and provide management information on the status and progress of the programme. Any training needs for the individuals appointed are identified and appropriate training courses scheduled.

Set up the processes and procedures required to manage the programme

Procedures are defined that will be implemented and managed by the Programme Support Office using existing corporate standards if available. Corporate standards may require tailoring to suit the particular needs of the programme. The Programme Support Office procedures should include the following:
- configuration management – covering all documents, deliverables, baselines and events
- planning – defining the content and level of detail required for the plans
- tracking and reporting – including project reporting
- communications management
- quality management
- risk management
- issues management – establish the programme's Issues Log and define how issues raised across the programme will be centrally controlled and managed.

The programme standards that will be followed throughout the programme are confirmed. These standards should include:
- Human Resource policies, including the relationships between members of the Programme Management team and staff in the rest of the organisation(s)
- technology standards for the IT systems and facilities that will be required by the programme. A specific responsibility for ensuring the integrity of these standards may be assigned to a 'Design Authority' or 'Compliance Management' function

- procurement and contract management policies. Contract management procedures and responsibilities will be required to cover any procurement activities on the programme
- general business practices for the management of the programme.

Establish the benefits measurement processes

The programme must be able to measure the benefits achieved as a result of delivering the new capability. The Benefit Profiles define how the benefits will be measured. The mechanisms for measuring the benefits should be set up so that the 'before state' can be captured as well as the improved situation achieved as a result of the programme.

Set up the infrastructure and tools required to help manage the programme

Tools to support the Programme Support Office functions need to be acquired and implemented, such as:

- websites
- planning and scheduling tools
- estimating tools.

Establish the communications channels

The Communications Strategy defines the mechanisms the programme will use to inform the stakeholders about the programme and to encourage feedback into the programme. The required mechanisms are set up for communicating to all the identified stakeholders in the programme. It is useful to begin using the programme's communication channels by providing details to the stakeholders of all the individuals appointed to specific roles on the programme as early as possible.

14.3 Inputs, outputs and decisions

Table 15 shows the inputs, outputs and decisions for 'Establishing a Programme'.

Table 15: Inputs, outputs and decisions	Item	Type	Notes
	Benefits Management Strategy and Benefit Profiles	Input	Used to set up the measurement mechanisms and establish the 'before state' metrics
	Risk Management Strategy and Risk Log	Input	Document management and control procedures established
	Quality Management Strategy	Input	Document management and control procedures established
	Programme Plan	Input	Used to establish the management and control procedures for monitoring progress against the Plan
	Communications Strategy and Stakeholder Map	Input	Used to establish the communications channels for the programme

Programme Organisation Structure	Input	Personnel appointed and any required training scheduled
Programme Support Office tools and procedures	Output	Tools and procedures that will be managed and controlled by the Programme Support Office
Issues Log	Output	Used to capture and assess issues raised at the programme level
Programme standards, policies and procedures	Output	Established by the Programme Support Office

14.4 Responsibilities

Table 16 shows the responsibilities associated with 'Establishing a Programme'.

Table 16: Responsibilities

Role	Responsibility
Programme Director	Appointment of Programme Manager and ensuring the other roles for managing the programme are appointed
Programme Manager	Responsible for establishing the Programme Support Office and the programme's procedures and standards
Programme Support Office	Establishing the support tools and infrastructure for the programme

fifteen

MANAGING THE PROJECT PORTFOLIO

15.1 Purpose

The delivery from the projects within the Project Portfolio provides the organisation with the new capabilities defined in the Blueprint. The purpose of 'Managing the Project Portfolio' is to provide an effective monitoring and management regime for the projects so that their benefits are delivered according to the Programme Plan. The activities of this process are repeated as necessary for each tranche of projects.

15.2 Activities

Project delineation

The projects within the Project Portfolio are scoped and defined. For new projects, a Project Brief is developed for each project so that the project is as self-contained as possible. For existing projects that are already underway, their project documentation is reviewed, and any required amendments or re-scoping in order to align with the programme's Blueprint should be discussed and agreed with the Project Management teams. The objective is for each project to have a clear scope and boundary, and a measurable definition of its required deliverables or outcome. For each of the projects within the Portfolio, the following should be identified:

- brief description of the deliverable/outcome
- dependencies on other projects
- target delivery date
- cost profile
- resource profile
- Benefit Profile(s) relevant to the project.

The Dependency Network is developed, showing how each project's inputs and outputs are related to each other (see *Programme planning*, chapter 4, for details of the Dependency Network).

Project scheduling

The projects are grouped into tranches (for further information on tranches, see *Programme planning*, chapter 4) and the deliverables scheduled into the Programme Plan. The projects are scheduled by considering all their interfaces with other projects and any opportunities for sharing or pooling resources. Each tranche should complete at an identifiable point such that the programme can demonstrate delivery of some of the expected benefits. 'Early wins' often help the programme achieve stronger commitment and support. It may be useful to schedule a formal Programme Benefits Review at some of these points to assess the success (or otherwise) of the benefits identification, management and realisation processes and make any adjustments necessary.

The end of each tranche also provides a management control point for assessing the continued viability of the programme's Business Case and hence the activities of the programme. A formal decision may be taken whether to proceed with the next tranche, suspend the programme to allow for realignment or re-design, or potentially abandon the programme and re-allocate the resources on the remaining projects.

Refine the
Programme Plan

Any appropriate tolerances against time and cost variances are built into the Programme Schedule and the Programme Plan is refined. The Plan is updated as the programme progresses with actual completion and delivery dates for the project.

Project start up

The Programme Manager is responsible for commissioning projects within the Project Portfolio and should ensure the appropriate individuals are appointed to the Project Boards. The Project Board is ultimately accountable to the programme for the successful completion of the project within specified time, cost and quality parameters. As each project is about to begin, the Programme Manager discusses and agrees the Project Brief with the Project Management team. The Programme Support Office provides assistance to the projects in the development of their plans and reporting mechanism to the programme. Each project plan should include a schedule of regular progress reporting to allow tracking of the projects against the Programme Plan.

Monitor progress

Progress against the Programme Plan is monitored and tracked, using information provided by the projects. Project reports should align with the information held at the programme level. Any departures from previously published project plans are assessed for impact on the rest of the programme. The impact of any change within a project on other parties within the programme needs to be managed.

The 'live' projects are supervised by focusing on the areas forming the greatest risk to the programme, such as:

- *deliverables* – it is vital that the project deliverables meet the requirements of their 'customers', whether these comprise end users or other projects
- *timely completion* – each project must take responsibility for adhering to timely forecasts of delivery. This is required especially for deliverables supplied to other projects, which will otherwise be affected by slippages
- *risks* – projects within a programme comprise a mutually dependent network. It is important for the integrity of this network that project teams are open and honest about risks. A failure to recognise and track risks could jeopardise both other projects and the benefits expected from the programme
- *estimates* – the accuracy with which resource and cost estimation is carried out may be an important influence on the programme's Business Case. It may also affect other projects by reducing the level of shared resources unexpectedly.

The programme's documentation, is updated and maintained, especially the Blueprint and Programme Plan, as the programme progresses, and at least at the end of each tranche of projects. Successive refinements to the Blueprint will highlight any adjustments that need to be made to the Portfolio.

Project closure	The process of project closure is supported, reflecting any lessons learned across subsequent projects. The project teams are assisted in the closure of their projects, including the formal hand-over of the deliverable or outcome. The Post Project Reviews should be scheduled to fit into the Programme Benefit Review process.
Communication	Throughout the running of the programme, it is vital to maintain communications across the projects and with the various stakeholders.

15.3 Inputs, outputs and decisions

Table 17 shows the inputs, outputs and decisions associated with 'Managing the Project Portfolio'.

Table 17: Inputs, outputs and decisions	Item	Type	Notes
	Blueprint	Input	Updated and refined as projects deliver
	Programme Plan	Input	Updated with the detailed schedule of projects and refined as projects deliver
	Benefit Profiles	Input	Updated and monitored
	Project Lessons Learned Reports	Output	As each project closes, these are distributed across the remaining projects within the Portfolio
	Project Briefs	Output	For commissioning new projects within the Portfolio
	Risk Log	Input	Used to monitor risks associated with project delivery, updated as projects deliver
	Project progress reports	Input	Used to monitor progress and update Programme Plan and Blueprint
	End of tranche review	Decision	Management decision to proceed, re-align or potentially abandon the programme
	Communication Plan	Input	Updated as programme progresses

15.4 Responsibilities

Table 18 shows the responsibilities associated with 'Managing the Project Portfolio'.

Table 18: *Responsibilities*	Role	Responsibilities
	Programme Manager	Responsible for the overall progress of the Project Portfolio and monitoring against the Programme Plan and Blueprint
	Project Board	Delivery of project to the programme
	Programme Director	Ongoing decision-making for the programme and advising the Programme Manager
	Sponsoring Group	Input at major decision points on the programme, such as reviews at end of tranches
	Programme Support Office	Operating the programme information management system and providing advice and support to the Programme Manager. Advice to projects on planning and reporting
	Business Change Manager	Responsible for ensuring the projects' deliverables can be readily integrated into the operational areas concerned so that benefit realisation can be achieved

sixteen

DELIVERING BENEFITS

16.1 Purpose

The programme will deliver new capabilities, services or business operations. The purpose of 'Delivering Benefits' is to track the specific benefits that were identified at the start of the programme and drive through the process of realising benefits from the new capabilities, services or operations in measurable terms. This process requires the management of the transition between 'old' and 'new' ways of working.

16.2 Activities

Benefits monitoring

The project teams are briefed on their benefit responsibilities and reporting requirements for the programme. As the programme progresses, project costs, issues and risks affecting both project and programme delivery are tracked.

Throughout the programme, progress against the Programme Plan is reviewed and delivery of the Blueprint tracked to identify potential improvements to benefits achievement. The Benefits Profiles and Benefits Plan are adjusted to reflect any such changes. Adjustments may be identified from a range of different events, such as:
- projects are not progressing to plan
- the business operations that will use the project's deliverables are unstable
- forward plans are no longer realistic based on experience to date
- external circumstances have changed affecting the future course of the programme
- the perception of the programme's objectives has changed.

Throughout the programme, the project teams need to be advised on any impact affecting their benefit responsibilities. The Lessons Learned Reports from the projects may be useful to inform this activity.

Measuring benefits

The Benefits Management Strategy and the individual Benefit Profiles define how each benefit will be measured. Measuring benefits should focus on assessing the improvement in performance of the business operations from the 'before state' and should be able to identify the improvements that are achieved as the new capability becomes integrated into the business operations.

Communication

It is vital to maintain communications across the projects and with the various stakeholders about the benefits expected from the programme.

Benefits realisation

As each project approaches its closure, the quality of the outcome or deliverable and its 'fitness for purpose' are confirmed. Not every project within the portfolio will deliver outcomes directly contributing to the Blueprint. Some projects are providing pre-requisites for other projects. By definition, these projects are not directly linked to benefits realisation.

Transition management — The relevant business operations are prepared for delivery of the project's outcome and the project's handover to the business operations facilitated. Performance measurement of the relevant business operations should be established, to assess improvements made as a result of the delivered change.

Updating the Blueprint — As a new capability is delivered into the business operations, the Blueprint and Benefits Plan should be updated to reflect the change and assess any impact on future benefits realisation.

16.3 Inputs, outputs and decisions

Table 19 shows the inputs, outputs and decisions associated with 'Delivering Benefits'.

Table 19:
Inputs, outputs and decisions

Item	Type	Notes
Benefit Profiles	Input	Adjusted to reflect changes
Programme Plan	Input	Used to monitor progress
Project progress reports and lessons learned reports	Input	Used to identify impact on benefits
Benefits Plan	Input	Used to monitor progress and updated to reflect achievements
Improvements to the business operations	Output	Measured improvements as a result of delivery of new capability
Blueprint	Input	Used to identify which business operations will realise the benefits, and then updated to reflect the change

16.4 Responsibilities

Table 20 shows the responsibilities associated with 'Defining Benefits'.

Table 20:
Responsibilities

Role	Responsibility
Business Change Manager	Delivery of project outcomes into the business (transition management) and realisation of the benefits by business operations.
Programme Manager	Adjusting Project Portfolio to optimise benefits delivery. Updating and maintaining programme documentation
Programme Director	Resolution of conflicts and approval of changes affecting course of programme

seventeen
CLOSING A PROGRAMME

17.1 Purpose

Programmes tend to last for many months and typically a few years. There is often a danger of allowing the programme to drift on, as if it is part of 'normal business'. The purpose of 'Closing a Programme' is to ensure the focus is on achieving the 'end-goal' of the programme, formally recognising when the programme has completed its Portfolio of projects and delivered the required new capability defined in the Blueprint. Benefits will have been delivered and realised along the way; however, the majority of major business benefits may not be fully realised until some time after the last project has delivered its outcome. This process identifies the need for future assessments of benefit realisation as well as a review of those achieved so far.

17.2 Activities
Confirming project closure

The programme confirms that all projects within the portfolio have been formally closed, and any remaining hand-over activities have been defined and assigned to relevant business operations. If the programme is being closed prematurely (that is, before the Blueprint is achieved), the remaining 'live' projects that are still required by the organisation need to be re-assigned to business management or perhaps to another programme.

Programme Benefits Reviews

A formal Programme Benefits Review should be conducted to assess the performance of the programme and identify lessons learned that may benefit other programmes. This Review should include an assessment of the management processes of the programme itself, as well as the level of achievement of the Blueprint, and the benefits that have already been delivered and realised. Some benefits may not yet have been realised; however, the ability to realise the benefit should be available and ready to be implemented.

A further Review should be scheduled for an appropriate point after closure of the programme – the Post Programme Review. This Review should assess the success of the programme's entire benefits realisation process, including those benefits that may not have been ready for measurement and assessment when the programme closed. The Post Programme Review should be scheduled when the transformed organisation has reached a 'steady state' and the changes delivered by the programme have become established into the business operations. To reinforce the work of the programme, a continuous improvement philosophy should be established so that the organisation is able to encourage further benefit achievement and improvements in performance.

Update and finalise programme documentation

Programme documentation should be reviewed to ensure that any issues, risks and outstanding actions have been attended to appropriately.

Disband programme management and support functions	The programme's infrastructure and management processes, are disbanded including releasing individuals from their appointed roles. Any contracts used by the programme, are finalised and closed, or the responsibility for the contracts handed over to business management.
Inform stakeholders	Programme closure is confirmed with the Programme Director and programme sponsors. All stakeholders need to be informed of programme closure and should be provided with relevant information about the programme's outcome, the new procedures and operations, and any other relevant changes to the organisation that were delivered by the programme.

17.3 Inputs, outputs and decisions

Table 21 shows the inputs, outputs and decisions associated with 'Closing a Programme'.

Table 21: Inputs, outputs and decisions

Item	Type	Notes
All programme documentation	Input	Reviewed and formally closed and filed
Confirmation of programme closure	Output	Formal notification to the stakeholders of programme closure
Programme Benefits Review	Output	Assessment of the programme itself and the benefits delivered so far. Planned date for the Post Programme Review should be set during this review

17.4 Responsibilities

Table 22 shows the responsibilities associated with 'Closing a programme'.

Table 22: Responsibilities

Role	Responsibility
Programme Director	Chair Benefits Review, release of personnel from programme management team, sign-off for programme closure
Sponsoring Group	Sign-off, release of Programme Director
Programme Manager	Closure of programme documentation, disbanding programme infrastructure
Business Change Manager	Assessment of achievement of benefits realised at this point and establishing ongoing performance measures

ANNEXES

RISK IDENTIFICATION CHECKLIST

This annex provides a checklist of questions to assist in the identification of risks.

Strategic level risks

What are the risks emerging from the environment in which the business operates and the environment in which programmes are run?

Other programmes

Existing programmes may both be a source of risk to a new programme and offer the benefit of experience for identifying risks:

- what analysis of risk has already been carried out?
- has the analysis of risk from legacy programmes been realistically reviewed?
- what has gone wrong in the past and what lessons can be learned from those experiences?
- are new inter-programme dependencies created?

Other initiatives within the organisation

If a new initiative arises during the course of a programme, it is important to work through the impact of the new initiative on the programme:

- is it possible to revise the programme to accommodate the new initiative?
- if not, what are the impacts of delaying the new initiative's introduction or introducing it as a separate programme?

Inter-programme dependencies

Although they are often difficult to anticipate, dependencies between programmes should be carefully considered.

- have all known inter-programme dependencies been identified and considered?

Political pressures

Are political pressures on the programme well understood and documented?

- have they been regularly revisited through the life of the programme?
- what risks threaten successful management of the programme?

Programme level risks
Changing requirements and objectives

If objectives are vague the programme is likely to be exposed to considerable dangers during implementation, especially if a new initiative causes the programme's objectives to alter:

- have the sponsors reached a genuine consensus on the objectives for the programme?
- can the objectives be quantifiably defined, so that success can be measured later?

Programme definition

Risk is inherent in planning a programme:

- does the programme call for any divergence from organisational standards?
- have the stakeholders been involved in defining and planning the programme?
- have approval and sign-off procedures been set in place?

Management skills	Ensure that the logical roles identified for managing the programme are appropriately tailored and made the clear responsibility of named individuals: • are in-house skills available? • are third party providers required to be contracted in to assist management of the programme?
Inter-project dependencies	The Programme Manager is responsible for defining and monitoring inter-project dependencies: • are the inter-dependencies between projects clearly defined? • what risks may affect the conduct of projects?
Project level risks *Project risks*	To manage the risks to projects well, it is necessary to: • ensure each Project Brief outlines these risks from the perspective of the programme • as individual projects progress, feedback should be provided to the programme's risk analysis and management activities.
Third party resources	It may be expected that a lack of skills in-house can be met by bringing them in from outside. Careful thought should be given to what bundles of products and services are to be provided by third parties: • is there difficulty in drawing up exact Terms of Reference, specifications and contracts? • can win-win relationships be established with service providers or are they likely to be adversarial? • is there pressure to contract out core management tasks? • has enough time been allowed for procurement of external resources? • is the management of third parties and the associated contract management function understood and resourced?
Operational level risks *Transfer of deliverables to operations*	Transition must be properly planned, managed and resourced. There may be projects to deliver soft outcomes (for example changes in staff behaviour) as well as physical deliverables: • are there constraints that limit proper piloting and testing? • are expectations realistic? • what risks arise from handing over project deliverables to the business and bringing in change with new systems or new ways of working?
Acceptability within business operations	Business managers must be involved in the benefits identification and management processes: • have the relevant business managers been identified, whose areas will be affected by the outcome of the programme? • how are they involved in identifying and realising the benefits to the business through improved performance of their operations?

Acceptability to stakeholders

The same considerations apply to the programme's stakeholders:

- are stakeholders' requirements understood and reflected in the programme's aims and objectives?
- are the stakeholders suitably involved within the programme?

PROGRAMME DOCUMENTATION OUTLINES

The following outlines provide a suggested content for the major Programme Management documents described in this guide.

Blueprint	*Purpose*	Describes the way the organisation will deliver the capabilities described in the Vision Statement. Used to maintain the programme's focus on delivering the required transformation and benefits during the lifetime of the programme
	Composition	Business model of functions, processes and decision-making operations
		Operational measures of costs, performance, service levels for the transformed organisation
		Organisation structure, staffing levels, roles and skills for the transformed organisation.
		Information systems, tools, equipment and other facilities required for the transformed organisation.
		Support services, costs, performance, service levels to enable the transformed organisation operate efficiently and effectively
	Derivation	Vision Statement Programme Mandate and Programme Brief
Benefits Management Strategy	Purpose	Defines how the programme will identify, monitor, deliver and realise the expected benefits. Used to monitor the delivery of business benefits throughout the programme.
	Composition	Benefits Plan showing the schedule of when benefits will fall in-line with projects delivery plans Benefits review and measurement process

	Derivation	Vision Statement Blueprint Programme Plan
Benefit Profile	*Purpose*	Used to track benefits delivery and realisation
	Composition	Description of benefit Financial valuation of the benefit (where possible) Changes to business operations/staffing Dependencies (on projects, risks, other, benefits and programmes, etc) Project responsible for delivery When the benefit will be delivered Which business area is responsible for realisation Timescale for realisation Key performance indicators Measurement process
	Derivation	Vision Statement Blueprint
Business Case	*Purpose*	Defines the justification for undertaking the programme, based on the estimated costs of the programme and the anticipated benefits to the organisation as a result of the transformed organisation and its new/extended capability
	Composition	Reasons Benefits Risks Costs and timescales Investment appraisal (if appropriate)
	Derivation	Business strategy and/or Programme Brief Blueprint and Vision Statement Programme Plan
Communications Strategy	*Purpose*	Defines how information about the programme will be disseminated to stakeholders, people directly involved in the programme, the rest of the organisation, and

		any other external organisations. Defines how people will be able to feed back their views, issues, ideas into the programme. Used to establish and manage the ongoing communications about the programme
	Composition	Communication mechanisms to be used, such as seminars, videos, email Key elements of programme information to be disseminated How information from stakeholders, etc will be received and handled within the programme Roles and responsibilities of key individuals involved in the programme Communications Plan showing when the activities will happen
	Derivation	Stakeholder Map Blueprint and Vision Statement Programme Plan
Financial Plan	*Purpose*	To provide the basis for financial management and control throughout the programme
	Composition	Accounting procedures for costs and expenditure Budget for programme activities Cost and expenditure profile across the programme Project cost and expenditure plans Approval points
	Derivation	Programme Plan Business Case Blueprint Project Portfolio
Programme Brief	*Purpose*	To define the programme's objectives, in outline, for approval to proceed to define the programme in detail
	Composition	Background Vision Statement

		Benefits expected
		Known risks
		Estimate of overall effort required
	Derivation	Business strategy and/or Programme Mandate
Programme Organisation Structure	*Purpose*	To document the roles and responsibilities, including appointed individuals, for all personnel involved in management and support activities on the programme
	Composition	Organisation structure including programme and project interfaces Roles and responsibilities Staff management issues, such as personnel performance reviews
	Derivation	Existing organisational structures Project Portfolio Blueprint
Programme Plan	*Purpose*	To define the programme's schedule for projects and benefits delivery. Used throughout the programme to track and monitor progress
	Composition	List of projects Benefits (and dis-benefits) expected Costs Risks and Issues Resources required Overall schedule for programme
	Derivation	Blueprint
Project Portfolio	*Purpose*	To list the projects that are or will be part of the programme
	Composition	Project list Outline project information such as target timescales, resources required
	Derivation	Blueprint

Quality Management Strategy	Purpose	Defines how the deliverables from the programme management team and the projects will be assessed for quality. Used by the project teams within their quality management processes. Used by the programme management team to plan the reviews of the programme documentation
	Composition	Quality control, assurance and audit processes to be applied to programme and project deliverables Quality review processes to be applied to programme and project deliverables Change management and control procedures for programme deliverables Key quality criteria for programme and project deliverables Corporate or industry standards to be met
	Derivation	Corporate Quality Management System Industry standards Programme Plan
Risk Log	*Purpose*	To track and monitor risks to the programme and its potential for delivering the required benefits
	Composition	Risk definition Impact on programme Likelihood Countermeasures Current status
	Derivation	Blueprint Benefit Profiles Project Portfolio Programme Plan
Risk Management Strategy	*Purpose*	Defines how risks will be managed during the lifecycle of the programme. Used to plan the way risks are handled within the programme
	Composition	What risks are to be managed How much risk is acceptable

		Who is responsible for the risk management activities
		What relative significance time, cost, benefits, quality, stakeholders have in the management of programme risks
	Derivation	Programme Plan Blueprint Stakeholder Map
Stakeholder Map	*Purpose*	Identifies all interested parties both inside and outside the programme; may also include individuals or groups outside the business. Used to ensure that all stakeholder interests are catered for by the programme, including keeping them informed and receiving feedback
	Composition	Matrix showing individual stakeholders or groups of stakeholders and their particular interests in the programme
	Derivation	Blueprint Programme Plan Organisational structures of organisations involved in the programme
Vision Statement	*Purpose*	Describes the outcome of the programme in terms of new or extended capability of the transformed organisation. Delivery of this capability is the end-goal of the programme
	Composition	Description of the capabilities the organisation seeks to achieve from the programme including performance measures, service levels, costs
	Derivation	Business strategy and core values Programme Mandate

FURTHER INFORMATION

The Office of Government Commerce develops guidance covering many topic areas including Strategic Management, Managing Information, Acquisition, Managing Services, Managing Performance, IT Service Management, Project Management, Business Continuity Management and many more. Full details of all published guidance are available on request.

Best Practice

Office of Government Commerce
Rosebery Court
St.Andrews Business Park
Norwich NR7 0HS

Telephone   +44 (0) 1603 704567
Email   info@ogc.gov.uk
Website   www.ogc.gov.uk

The APM Group Limited, on behalf of OGC, administers the accredited training scheme for Programme Management. Full details of all training providers are available on request.

APM Group Limited
7-8 Queen Square
High Wycombe
Buckinghamshire HP11 2BP

Telephone   +44 (0) 1494 452450
Facsimile   +44 (0) 1494 459559
Website   www.apmgroup.co.uk

GLOSSARY

Baseline   A product (typically a document) or set of products (or documents) which form a snapshot of a position or situation. Although the position maybe updated later on, under formal change control, the baseline remains unchanged and available as a reminder of the original state and as a comparison against the current position.

Benefit   The measurable improvement to existing and new business operations and services.

Benefit Manager   An optional role for assisting the Business Change Manager.

Benefit Profile   The definition of an individual benefit to the organisation including the mechanisms for measurement of the benefit.

Benefits management   A formal process within Programme Management for planning, managing, delivering and measuring the set of benefits which the programme is to deliver.

Benefits Management Strategy   The definition of how the programme will identify, deliver and realise the expected benefits from the programme. This is one of the most important pieces of programme documentation.

Benefits Plan   Shows when the expected benefits will fall during or after the programme.

Blueprint   Description of the transformed organisation which will be the result of the programme including the intermediate milestone points along the way. The Blueprint includes business models, operational performance measures, organisation, information systems and support service requirements.

Business Case   The justification for the commitment of resources to a programme, answering the question 'Why are we doing this programme?' The Business Case should enable the Programme Management team to select or adopt the most cost-effective combination of projects. It also provides the wider context and justification for infrastructure investment such as the costs of implementing new policies and standards.

Business Change Manager   The role responsible for enabling the organisation to realise the benefits delivered by the programme.

Capability   The term used to describe a new or enhanced business process, product or service that the organisation uses to achieve measurable benefit.

Change control	The formal process of managing and controlling changes to documents and deliverables produced by the programme and its projects.
Communications Manager	An optional role for assisting the Programme Manager.
Communications Plan	The detailed plan of when, what, how and with whom, the information flows will be established and maintained throughout the programme.
Communications Strategy	The definition of how the programme's objectives, plans and progress are to be communicated to the various stakeholders involved in the programme, and how the stakeholders' views and input will be received by the programme.
Configuration management	In the context of Programme Management, the process of identifying and controlling programme documentation such that it reflects the current state of the programme and the business operations.
Deliverable	An output, whether a tangible product or an intangible outcome, from a project or programme which is intended for use within the organisation, or within a project or by other projects within the programme. Another name often used for a deliverable is 'product'.
Dependency Network	A representation of the various project outcomes showing how each relates to the others in terms of pre-requisite or dependency.
Design Authority	An optional role that may be established by the Programme Manager with responsibility for • ensuring the consistency and integrity of the business organisation, processes and procedures that are to be created or changed as part of the programme • for ensuring the infrastructure and/or technical environment that will be required to support the new business complies with the policies and standards of the organisation.
Dis-benefit	An unfavourable outcome as a result of the programme's activities.
EFQM Excellence Model	Part of EFQM (European Foundation for Quality Management) standard for defining business processes.
Finance Manager	An optional role to assist the Programme Manager prepare and manage the programme's Financial Plan and manage the programme's expenditure.
Financial Plan	The detailed financial management and accounting practices for the programme, including the cost and expenditure profiles.

Infrastructure	The term used to describe the 'traditional' forms of infrastructure such as IT, telecommunications, buildings, as well as supporting services such as accountancy, human resources.
Issues Log	The central log of all reported issues facing the programme used to assist the process of managing the issues such that they do not adversely affect the programme.
Lessons Learned Report	Information provided by the projects on things that went well and things that went badly during the project.
Post Programme Review	The review of the programme's achievements in terms of realised benefits that is scheduled for a point where the organisation will have reached a 'steady state' after the change process.
Post Project Review	A review scheduled after the project has completed where the impact of the project's deliverables on the organisation can be assessed.
PRINCE2	OGC's project management method providing a process-based framework for setting up and controlling projects. PRINCE2 has defined interfaces to Programme Management.
Products	Assets, deliverables, or outcomes which have sufficient significance to the organisation or the programme such that they require controlled identification, review, and change control.
Programme	The portfolio of projects that are selected or commissioned, planned and managed in a co-ordinated way and which together achieve a set of defined business objectives.
Programme Assurance	The process of confirming to the programme's sponsoring group that the programme is being managed effectively and that the programme is delivering the desired outcome and benefits.
Programme Benefits Review (PBR)	A review to assess achievement of targets and to measure performance levels in the resulting business operations. A PBR may also be used to analyse success and failure in the Programme Management process. The PBR that is scheduled for after the programme has completed and closed is referred to as the Post Programme Review.
Programme Board	A steering committee representing the role of Programme Director where a single individual is not sufficiently empowered to direct the programme.
Programme Brief	Document describing the business objectives and vision for the programme that triggers the 'Defining a Programme' process.
Programme Definition	The total set of information that defines what the programme is going to achieve and how it is going to achieve it.

Programme Director	Role responsible for the overall success of the programme. The Programme Director provides strategic direction and executive decision making for the programme, and for managing relations with internal and external stakeholders.
Programme Management	The co-ordinated management of a portfolio of projects that change organisations to achieve benefits that are of strategic importance.
Programme Manager	The role responsible for day-to-day management of the programme according to the Programme Plan.
Programme Mandate	Defines the overall objectives for the programme and positions the programme within the organisation's corporate mission, goals, strategies and other initiatives. It is the trigger for Programme Management.
Programme Plan	Description of how the programme will deliver the Blueprint and when benefits can be realised.
Programme Schedule	The representation of the projects within a programme grouped into tranches.
Programme Support Office	The organisation providing technical support and administrative services to the programme, in particular management information reporting. The Programme Support Office may also provide support for the projects within the programme.
Project Board	The group responsible for direction setting and ultimate accountability for a project.
Project Brief	The reasons for the project, an outline Business Case, and the initial definition of project scope and objectives.
Project Executive	The role responsible for the successful delivery of a project's defined outcome. In PRINCE2, the Project Executive chairs the Project Board.
Project Initiation Document (PID)	The PRINCE2 definition of all the information about a project to enable management decisions to be made at the start and at intermediate points during a project.
Project Management	The framework, organisation and processes used to manage projects.
Project Manager	The individual responsible for the day-to-day management of a project. The Project Manager on a PRINCE2 project reports to the Project Board.
Project Plan	The description of the project's activities including a schedule of when they will happen and what each activity will deliver.

Project Portfolio	The collection of projects within a programme defined by their Project Briefs, time-scales and resources.
Quality management	The processes of ensuring quality is built in to the Programme Management processes and the programme's deliverables.
Quality Management Strategy	The statement of how quality will be built into the management of the programme and its outputs.
Quality Manager	An optional role for assisting the Programme Manager.
Risk Log	A central log of the identified risks to a programme (and potentially the risks to the projects within the programme) providing complete management information about the risks and their status at any point in time.
Risk Management Strategy	A detailed definition of how risks will be identified, analysed and managed on the programme.
Risk Manager	An optional role for assisting the Programme Manager.
Senior Supplier	One of the roles on a PRINCE2 Project Board responsible for committing specialist resources to the project.
Senior User	One of the roles on a PRINCE2 Project Board responsible for the interests of users.
Sponsoring Group	The group of senior executives involved in a programme. The sponsoring group may include executives from different organisations.
Stakeholder	An individual or group of individuals such as employees, directors, shareholders, service providers, consultants, external organisations who have an interest in the programme whether through their involvement with the programme or because they will be impacted by its outcome.
Stakeholder management	The processes involved in identifying, analysing and managing the expectations of stakeholders and their particular interests and needs.
Stakeholder Map	A matrix showing each stakeholder against their particular interest or need.
Tranche	A group of projects that represent the delivery of all or a recognisable part of a new capability. Tranches are used to assist the management and control of a programme.
Vision Statement	The customer-facing definition of what the programme is to deliver.

INDEX